I Don't Want to
Talk About It

by Terrance Real
(re: male depression)   per
                        Lupe

Awakening from Depression

With respect for the past and hope for the future,
we dedicate this book to our parents and to our children.

Awakening from Depression

By
Jerome Marmorstein, M.D.
Nanette Marmorstein

Woodbridge Press
Santa Barbara, California 93160

1993

Published by
Woodbridge Press Publishing Company
Post Office Box 6189
Santa Barbara, California 93160

Distributed simultaneously in the United States and Canada.

Printed in the United States of America.

Library of Congress Cataloging in Publication Data:

Marmorstein, Jerome.
   Awakening from depression : a mind / body approach to emotional recovery, by Jerome Marmorstein, Nanette Marmorstein.
      p.   cm.
   "Includes revised text from The Psychometabolic blues, by Jerome Marmorstein and Nanette Marmorstein, Woodbridge Press"—T.p. verso.
      ISBN 0-88007-190-7 : $9.95
      1. Depression, Mental—Popular works. 2. Depression—Mental—Physiological aspects.   3. Depression, Mental—Treatment.   4. Diet therapy. 5. Anxiety. I. Marmorstein, Nanette. II. Title.
RC537.M36 1991
616.85'27—dc20   91-27523
                                                              CIP

Table of Contents

Preface

All of us go through periods when we just don't feel well, often for no apparent reason. If we happen to have fever, pain, or a specific organic symptom, we're likely to consult a physician, especially if these symptoms don't clear up promptly by themselves.

But what can you do if you or a loved one just doesn't feel right, with little or no concrete symptoms to guide you? You may just lack the energy or desire to do the things you used to enjoy, or life may just seem monotonous, without purpose or meaning. Some may be experiencing too much nervous energy, driving themselves restlessly so that they can't relax, concentrate, or even sleep. Others may be experiencing a variety of persistent physical symptoms but feel embarrassed when repeated medical examinations and tests fail to demonstrate any definite reasons for their disturbances. What can you do for yourself or a loved one under these circumstances, and how can you tell when some kind of professional help is needed, and, if so, what kind?

Supplying practical effective solutions for these types of problems is the primary purpose of this book. Our recommendations have been developed over many years to fill the practical needs of a general internal medical physician's practice. Here, as is true for most general or family physicians, considerably more time was required to unravel so-called functional problems than those that can be more easily identified and confirmed with specific X-ray or laboratory findings.

Because these problems lack physical tangibility, it became necessary to develop a system of communication to accurately diagnose which of the "psychometabolic blues" one is dealing with: depression, anxiety, functional hypoglycemia, or functional fatigue. For this purpose we have developed a diagnostic depression-anxiety chart with numerical scoring to help you and your physician determine whether or not you might be suffering from anxiety or depression.

Perhaps the key to understanding the psychometabolic

blues lies in its very name. All of us have grown up at a time when terms like *psychological* and *mental* were interpreted as meaning little or no involvement of bodily physiology and chemistry. A new term, *psychometabolic*, recognizes that psychological and metabolic factors are integrated together through common biochemical and neurologic pathways to account for emotional feelings and behavior.

From a practical viewpoint, there wouldn't seem to be much purpose in finding out what's really wrong with you or a loved one if prompt effective solutions were not readily available. Therefore, this book is strongly devoted to helping you to overcome these disturbing conditions if they should occur, and to become the healthy self-reliant individual that you were meant to be.

Even when the word *we* is used in this book, keep in mind that responsibility for all professional and technical information, including possible erroneous conclusions, belongs to the physician half of this writing team.

Jerome and Nanette Marmorstein
Santa Barbara, California

CHAPTER 1

The Psychometabolic Blues and Why You May Have Them

With so many publications available to try to help you to overcome depression and find happiness, why spend your valuable time and money to read yet another book that you suspect will tell you again to love and assert yourself and not be concerned about the feelings of others? Anyway, isn't happiness just a question of making up one's mind to change certain unhealthy attitudes and habits?

To start with, no book can deliver happiness by itself; that's something you'll have to achieve for yourself, perhaps with some skilled assistance. If any previous publication or organization had succeeded in packaging happiness, there wouldn't have been so many others attempting to accomplish the same thing. And the long-held myth that emotional health and happiness are just a matter of overcoming unhealthy attitudes and behavior, without taking into consideration the role of chemical effects on the brain and body, has impaired the efficiency of emotional therapy for years. Thus, this book will take a different approach from others you may have read—for a variety of reasons.

First of all, the source of advice to help you to achieve emotional health is realistically based on the fertile experience of a general internist's medical practice. In this case, personal attention was not limited to psychological factors, but also included the opportunity to uncover potent treatable metabolic, chemical, and drug factors. These physical factors interact with the psychological ones to account for the full spectrum of the psychometabolic blues: anxiety, depression, functional fatigue, hypoglycemia, and such related "epidemics" as alcohol and drug abuse, disrupted family life, and irrational fears of illness and aging. This interaction is the rationale for coining the term *psychometabolic*. In addition, using this term serves to overcome the prejudice and distortion that have often been associated with such words as mental, emotional, or psychosomatic.

The most frequent correctable biochemical offenders are a variety of common, naturally occurring, previously unsuspected food, drink, and drug components. They have the power to disturb the normal functioning of the body and brain, either by themselves, or especially when accompanied by psychological stress as well. Knowledge of these factors may provide additional help for those who have already received other forms of psychological assistance. Also, these physical factors are simple to utilize, since they are few in number and easy to identify. And lastly, any additional psychological adjustments will be much easier to accomplish once the chemical interference with normal mental functioning has first been eliminated. With the exception of full-blown clinical depression or severe anxiety, the simplicity of this approach is enhanced in that it is usually unnecessary to add other medication. This has allowed a great reduction in our prescribing of tranquilizers, as well as a large reduction in the average dosage of antidepressant medication.

Regular physical exercise is a beneficial metabolic factor which, when used with our other recommendations, completes a simple and surprisingly effective physical regimen, sufficient for some conditions alone, or as a corollary to necessary psychological changes in others.

This book also differs from most others in that it doesn't limit itself to just the metabolic or just the psychological factors. Since our conclusions are not preconceived by allegiance to any particular school of psychology, the resulting approach is a total one, where physical and psychological factors are dealt with as a unified interaction involving the whole person. Furthermore, the practical demands of a busy general internal medical practice require an orderly, systematic approach offering accurate diagnosis and effective, prompt results. This has usually been achieved within several weeks.

The psychological approach has been developed through

unbiased observation over years of dealing with emotional problems, as an integral part but not the totality of our medical responsibilities. Therefore, the setting and spectrum of these problems comes closer to the most common range of experiences than would be the case if one had specialized in just emotional conditions.

While the traditional approach of spending time analyzing one's past experiences may not always be necessary, there are situations where the complexity or severity of the emotional problems will require psychotherapy with a psychologist or psychiatrist. But even here the use of our physical and psychological recommendations will often provide additional benefits.

The "separateness" of the mind and the body is artificial, anyway. While the body's workings are conducted through large enough tubes and plumbing to be seen and felt, the mind, as contained in the brain, works on such an ultramicroscopic level that the electrochemical molecular changes cannot be visualized. So the resulting thoughts, feelings, and behavior seem to occur as if by some sort of magic.

By pointing out the most common physical and psychological roadblocks to emotional health, this book can help you to determine your own alternatives to overcoming or preventing these problems. These obstacles to emotional health and happiness are deeply rooted in our modern urbanized and industrialized way of living. Not that anxiety, depression, fatigue, and their resulting problems are new, but their incidence has risen to epidemic proportions in the past decade and this in turn must be related to prevailing customs and habits involving not only how we eat, drink, and exercise, but also how we live our lives psychologically and socially.

It may seem simplistic to link much of our social, family, and personal problems to anxiety and depression, but this approach has been practical and effective in actual practice. It should also help you prevent or overcome such problems as alcohol, drug, and food addictions; compulsive overwork; undue fear of physical illness; marital and sexual disappointments; family disruption; antisocial behavior; persistent guilt and anger; and exaggerated, unreasonable fear of aging and death.

As we said, our broad-based approach may seem rather simplistic. Yet, it may have been dependency on fractionalized statistics and laboratory experiments that has failed to adequately explain the complex nature of individual human behavior. As important as statistics and experimentation are for education and research about diseased organs, when dealing with individual human beings, group generalizations must take a back seat to the consideration of each person as the unique, total individual that he or she is. A totally committed, personalized approach is the format in which the approach in this book has been developed.

The long-term health of the individual, both physical and emotional, is the reference point that is repeatedly applied in this book. The priority of health serves to promote scientific objectivity and to avoid the confusion of unhealthy misconceptions. It also encourages individuals to be more responsible for their own well-being.

Using such an individualized approach requires adequate practical information to allow you to determine from which form of the psychometabolic blues you or a loved one may be suffering. Is it just a case of functional fatigue, with its accompanying lack of enthusiasm, that might promptly clear up with a few nutritional and exercise recommendations? Or could it actually be a full-blown clinical depression that would likely require professional assistance? Perhaps it's just temporary anxiety from occupational stress that will subside once a deadline is past. Or possibly it's the confusion of body chemistry with nervousness, called functional hypoglycemia.

A practical means of determining whether you or a loved one may be suffering from depression is found in Chapter 3. This is a *Rapid Diagnostic Depression-Anxiety Chart* designed to diagnose and estimate the severity of depression as well as any associated anxiety. It could help in deciding the relative urgency of seeking professional help and then assist your physician or therapist in making an evaluation.

If you're really in trouble, you need more than a friend. You need a competent professional to help you unravel the many physical and emotional symptoms of the depression. The most practical place to start is with your own family physician or internist. If you don't have one, or one with whom you can adequately communicate, Chapter 4 offers information to help you find such a physician.

For those whose emotional needs are complicated enough to warrant more specialized attention, a personal physician is usually in a good position to recommend the psychiatrist or psychologist most appropriate for your individual needs.

It is equally important for patients and physicians to understand each other's inherent communication problems in order to achieve their common goals of good health—not only for the patient but also for the physician. Physicians are, after all, not basically different from any other human beings. Their technical skills and serious responsibilities are only limited by their capacity for clear, emotionally supportive communication.

In this regard, we have found most valuable an attitude that we call "skeptical open-mindedness." This is the willingness to consider any possibility no matter how ridiculous or unpopular it may seem initially, but then to withhold its acceptance as fact until it can be adequately supported by positive evidence.

More than anything else, our approach is born of the greatest possible respect for our own and everyone else's individuality. No two of us are exactly alike. Yet we share such great similarities in biologic and psychologic properties that we can easily identify with each other's problems, provided that we can free ourselves sufficiently of group judgments to allow unbiased concern.

Mutual respect for everyone's individuality does not mean that we can love everyone. Love is a special emotion which, by definition of specialness, can be applied only to a limited number of people. To like people, to sincerely respect them as individuals with dignity, is the beginning of true human communication. It has been honest communication from person to person, and from our own unconscious-to-conscious self-awareness, that has allowed this book to be written.

CHAPTER 2

Feeling Better With Four Simple Nutritional and Exercise Steps

We'll call her Mrs. S., but you probably know her by a different name. She is forty-one years old, has been married for sixteen years, has two children, and suffers from a lack of energy, mild depression, and restlessness. Beginning to sound familiar? Most physicians see hundreds of people like her. Typically, the complaints are functional in origin, and include, alone or together, functional fatigue, depression, anxiety, and functional hypoglycemia. And just as typically, the treatment most often prescribed is a tranquilizer.

Definition of the Psychometabolic Blues

For want of a more appropriate name, we have linked together these common everyday problems and called them the *Psychometabolic Blues*. These include not only the four diagnostic categories just mentioned, but also a number of specific situations that often result in anxiety and depression, and that currently plague modern civilized societies. They also account for most of the problems that family physicians deal with in everyday practice. Since the causes often involve combinations of metabolic and psychological factors, the treatment must also include them. This not only involves our eating, drinking, drug, and exercise habits, but also our priorities of material success, group acceptance, and faddism over the need for human values, individuality and moderation.

Tranquilizers can be helpful, but they're also costly and,

occasionally, hazardous, especially for those prone to drug dependency. Sometimes they can even worsen an underlying depression. Over the years, we've developed an alternate method of treatment for these common problems that is safe, simple, inexpensive, often more effective, and from a busy physician's point of view, very practical. In addition, it promotes an increase in alertness and energy, rather than sedation and drowsiness.

Four Metabolic Steps

This approach was developed empirically out of many years of experience as a general internal medical physician, observing the natural effects of certain influences on emotional behavior. In time, this has led to the use of four practical metabolic steps, used to treat functional fatigue, anxiety, depression, and functional hypoglycemia. They are: (1) the avoidance of all caffeine (decaffeinated coffee or herb teas can be substituted); (2) limiting intake of sweets and refined sugars (but not fresh fruits); (3) limitation of alcohol to no more than one drink daily; (4) regular exercise—as little as a 20-minute walk daily.

Exactly why this regimen works is still a puzzle, but from a practical point of view, it is effective and simple to apply. We suspect that it affects the metabolism of several adrenalin-type hormones called biogenic amines, whose imbalance in the brain has been implicated in anxiety and depression.

Caffeine stimulates the brain and sympathetic nervous system by increasing the secretion of adrenaline and then reducing its subsequent breakdown. This promptly aggravates such anxiety or hypoglycemia-like symptoms as irritability, shakiness, palpitation, dizziness, sweating, and insomnia. In addition, caffeine's post-stimulation letdown exaggerates the symptoms of functional fatigue and depression. Unlike the promptness of caffeine's effect on anxiety or hypoglycemia, detecting improvement in depression and functional fatigue may require several weeks of caffeine abstention.

Caffeine surely has been the most overlooked and ignored of the metabolic factors affecting the emotions. A group of psychiatrists at the University of Michigan have also concluded that persons with emotional problems are hypersensitive to even small amounts of caffeine. Additionally, a group of psychiatrists at a mood disorder clinic in Pittsburgh have confirmed that caffeine reduces the effectiveness of tranquilizers and antidepressants.

Similarly, as will be discussed in more detail later, many hypoglycemic symptoms are due to excessive buildup of noradrenalin and adrenalin. Although excessive use of alcohol and other mind-sedating drugs exerts primarily a depressive effect on the brain, they also cause a rebound agitation and anxiety mediated by excessive sympathetic nervous system activity and buildup of adrenalin.

Regular exercise has a beneficial effect on all of the psychometabolic blues, allowing improvement in energy, anxiety, depression, and sense of well-being, both physically and emotionally. Exercise need not be vigorous but should be regular, daily or every other day. As little as a 20-minute uninterrupted walk is usually adequate, but any sports or calisthenics involving leg motions can be utilized.

For those interested in peak levels of physical fitness, a scientific study has shown that oxygen consumption is equal between those who jog 30 minutes three days a week, and those who just walk briskly for 40 minutes four days a week.

Caution is necessary, of course, before embarking on any exercise program, particularly for those with medical problems, especially cardiac or orthopedic problems—or people over age thirty. For these people, particularly if more vigorous exercises are being considered, such as jogging or rope-jumping, a medical checkup would be wise. Although yoga stretching exercises do not involve much leg motion, they can afford considerable muscle relaxation and a sense of well-being and can be combined with other types of exercise such as walking for maximum benefit.

The exact mechanisms by which regular exercise helps relieve anxiety, depression, and fatigue are unknown, but good results have also been noted by independent studies from the University of Virginia and the University of Wisconsin. In addition to the ability of exercise to increase oxygen uptake and relieve muscle tension, it probably exerts a synchronizing effect upon the various systems of the body that have become desynchronized from fatigue and tension.

Since all four of these disorders are similar in that they are aggravated by the same four metabolic factors, they must share common brain metabolic pathways. There need be no reason to delay applying these steps if you have any of these problems. In our own practice, for instance, we've been able to greatly reduce the use of tranquilizers since employing this regimen. And the results have been so consistent that if someone fails to make progress on this regimen, it is usually an indication that the problem may be due to some other cause.

This does not mean that under certain circumstances a tranquilizer for anxiety or muscle spasm may not be useful, and the use of antidepressant medication for depression can be of great value.

A Vicious Cycle

It is paradoxical that the more fatigued, anxious, depressed, or hypoglycemic one becomes, the more apt is he or she to increase the intake of caffeine and sweets for temporary stimulation, consume more alcohol to relax and, because of fatigue, not get enough regular exercise. This behavior is understandable because of the immediate but temporary gratification that these chemicals will afford, and it is not readily apparent that the overall effect of this vicious cycle is actually a worsening of the conditions. It is only after the person has been made aware of these relationships, and has had an opportunity to apply these steps for two to four weeks, that the effects can then become apparent.

Depression

Consider the case of a forty-six-year-old widow we'll call Mrs. J. On her first visit to the office, she insisted on bringing her companion into the examining room. This seemed strange for a person her age, but she quickly explained that she never allowed herself to be alone because she was afraid that she might drop dead at any moment. In addition, she felt that her life had become empty and meaningless. In other words, she was depressed and had not been able to rid herself of these feelings in spite of several years of psychotherapy by a competent psychologist. After a thorough physical examination and tests, she was reassured and advised to cut out the three cups of coffee that she drank each morning and to take a daily walk for twenty minutes. When seen one month later, she had improved noticeably, had even started to play tennis, and seemed to have become comfortable in being alone.

Although Mrs. J. made her recovery without the aid of drugs, which she refused, the use of an antidepressant medication can be very helpful. In our experience, utilizing the four steps above has allowed a large reduction in the dosage of antidepressant medication* required to be effective.

For a clinical depression, additional time for counseling and reassurance is required. But, like most general physicians, we don't have the time or the training to engage in prolonged psychoanalysis. For those who do require a psychiatrist or psychologist because of the complexity and severity of their symptoms, we don't hesitate to recommend these specialists.

For others, the general physician can start to be effective on the first visit by emphasizing several points. First, depression is not a form of insanity—there is usually no loss of contact with reality, as might be evidenced by delusions (false, bizarre beliefs) or hallucinations (seeing or hearing things that are not there). Furthermore, since one out of four people will at some time develop depression, it's a very common illness. Pointing out that the guilt that often accompanies the depression is usually found to be grossly exaggerated is very helpful.

Since depression is often characterized by pessimism and hopelessness, those suffering from it are repeatedly reminded that it is one of the most curable of all diseases.

It is usually unnecessary for physicians to discuss with patients the intricate details of their personal lives or psychological problems. Instead, it is often sufficient to be direct and point out, briefly, any obvious distortions occurring in their attitudes toward these problems. A brief inquiry as to how things are going at home or at work may at times get to the root of the problem. For those with major situational problems such as chronic marital difficulties, a psychologist or psychiatrist experienced in marriage counseling, or perhaps a licensed marriage and family counselor may be in order. For others, combining the four practical steps with common-sense support often allows people to solve their own problems.

*Not to be confused with tranquilizers, which can occasionally cause physical or psychological dependency and abuse, antidepressant medications are free of these risks because they work indirectly by allowing the brain to restore its own natural chemical balance.

Functional Fatigue

Since a persistent fatigue can result from any of a wide variety of physical and emotional illnesses, it is important to consult a physician for its evaluation. Nevertheless, much of the time no definite physical disease will be found, and the term *functional fatigue* can be used. In these cases, it often results from either transient stress, a recent viral illness, alcohol or drug effects, overwork, or improper nutrition and exercise, as discussed in the metabolic factors. Another major cause is the disease of depression, whose other symptoms will be discussed in the next chapter. Functional fatigue, either alone or with depression, is often unlike that which occurs as a result of physical disease, because it may be worse on awakening and improves during the day. Furthermore, it is not usually experienced as a true muscle weakness, but as a feeling of lethargy, sleepiness, or lack of enthusiasm.

Take the case of a forty-three-year-old businessman we'll call Mr. T. By the time he was seen, he had been through nearly a half dozen other doctors' offices in the previous two years. None of them had been able to discover the cause of nor help to cure the persistent fatigue that forced him to take to his bed several days each month. He had already been checked for hypoglycemia as well as other diseases, and had not improved on any regimen. There were no symptoms to suggest a major clinical depression. He was very surprised when he no longer needed to remain in bed from fatigue within four weeks after he eliminated all caffeine and began a daily exercise program of walking.

In recent years a new disorder called *chronic fatigue syndrome* has emerged. At first it was thought to be due to a prolonged bout with the virus causing infectious mononucleosis. That was the reason it was called *chronic Epstein-Barr virus syndrome.* Further studies have since disclosed that this is probably not the case but instead may be due to altered immunity associated with a variety of initial viral infections. The most common factor identified, however, has been depression. But it is not always clear if it is a cause or a result of the symptoms. These symptoms include low-grade fever, sore throat, swollen neck lymph nodes, fatigue, inability to concentrate, joint pains and a variety of other symptoms. After weeks or months or, rarely, years, almost all recover. Antidepressant medications are at times helpful.

Functional Hypoglycemia

Functional or reactive hypoglycemia is a frequent problem the exact nature of which is not totally understood. In fact, it has become a point of dispute between the medical establishment and many self-styled nutritional advocates. Whether the condition is just a manifestation of sugar and caffeine intolerance or is another form of anxiety is academic. The practical point is that avoiding concentrated sweets, caffeine, and excessive starches will usually be helpful. Some people may also need extra protein with and between meals.

Curiously, half of our patients with classic hypoglycemic symptoms of weakness, hunger, shakiness, and restlessness relieved by eating, have normal results from five-hour glucose tolerance tests rather than subnormal blood sugar some time after eating glucose sugar. However, both those with normal results and those with abnormal results respond favorably to restriction of carbohydrates and caffeine, with the occasional addition of protein. Furthermore, we consistently observe that the majority of those with anxiety, depression, and fatigue, whose symptoms are not even triggered by intake of sweets, still show improvement in their symptoms when they limit their intake of sugar and caffeine.

We suspect that the rapid drop in blood glucose that normally follows the rapid rise after eating refined sugars and sweets may be falsely interpreted by the body (as if it were the subnormal blood glucose level experienced by persons with anxiety, fatigue, or depression). Since the avoidance of concentrated sweets has usually been effective, whether or not the five-hour glucose tolerance test results are abnormal, this test would seem to be optional unless the person is also suspected of having diabetes mellitus, or has symptoms severe enough to suggest a possible organic cause. Therefore, a medical evaluation would be necessary to rule out such underlying physical causes as untreated early diabetes mellitus, or, rarely, thyroid, pituitary and adrenal insufficiency, pancreatic tumors, and liver disease. In these latter situations, the hypoglycemia would not be functional but organic, as would the low blood sugar resulting from excessive response to medications used to treat diabetes mellitus.

The low drop of blood sugar in functional hypoglycemia is usually due to excessive secretion of insulin by an otherwise normal pancreas. Although caffeine restriction is helpful for all those with anxiety, depression, and fatigue, it is especially important for those with symptoms of hypoglycemia.

Pseudo Hypoglycemia

A good example of pseudo hypoglycemia was Mrs. P. This thirty-five-year-old homemaker had come in complaining of fatigue, nervousness, insomnia, and shakiness relieved by having a sweet snack. For several years she had gotten into the habit of having candy or pastry between meals and found she also needed the temporary pickup from a cup of coffee several times a day. She had felt too tired to do any exercise. After a negative examination and normal five-hour glucose tolerance test, she quit caffeine and between-meal snacks but allowed herself fruit or sponge cake with her dinner. In addition, she either walked daily or played tennis. When seen a month later, she indicated that she had not felt so well for years. She was not seen again for several years, when she returned for an examination complaining of a recurrence of the same symptoms. She then realized that, while on a long trip, she had slipped into her old habits of using caffeine and sweets and avoiding exercise. Again, she was gratified to lose these symptoms within several weeks after resuming her former diet and exercise.

Alcohol

Of the four metabolic steps, the most difficult to change has been drinking habits. This is because of the dependency caused by using alcohol for its pharmacologic sedative effect upon the brain, and this develops among people who say that they need a drink to unwind, relax, or forget their problems. On the other hand, the limitation to only one drink of hard alcohol, beer or wine a day does not usually afford significant sedative effect on the brain. Here, the usage is for either a social ritual or as a complement of food. But when someone routinely seeks out the transient sedation or euphoria afforded by several drinks, he or she will be difficult to convince that the long-term effect may be one of increasing anxiety, fatigue, or depression.

Multiple Metabolic Factors

Mr. W., a rapidly rising young executive, found that the demands of his job prevented him from being able to relax when he finally got home in the evening. He found that one or two drinks did not continue to be sufficient, and was concerned when he found himself requiring a third one. He also found it necessary to increase his coffee consumption to six cups throughout the day in order to maintain enough energy to complete the demands of his job. While he had previously enjoyed regular sports and exercise, he no longer seemed to have the time or the enthusiasm for them. He became aware that he was no longer good company for his family. After completion of a normal physical exam and appropriate tests, he agreed to try quitting caffeine, limiting alcohol to no more than one drink a day, and to take at least a brief walk every lunchtime. When seen a month later, he was amazed at his increase of energy and ability to handle work demands without feeling overwhelmed or anxious.

Cocaine and Crack

Among the most addicting of all recreational drugs, cocaine—especially in its crack inhalation form—has become the focus of the major drug epidemic of recent times. Rapid addiction to cocaine and the serious problems associated with its use—depression and paranoid delusions as well as heart attacks and strokes—make it one of the most dangerous drugs known. It has been associated with the highest rate of teenage gang killings in American history.

Other Recreational Drugs

Other recreational drug use is also dangerous to mind and body. So-called "speed" includes stimulant drugs that have effects similar to those of cocaine. An inhaled form called "ice" is even more rapidly addicting—much like crack in that respect. In fact, all stimulant drugs and depressant drugs, whether illegal or legally available, can inflict great damage. Now that intravenous drug abuse with such substances as heroin or cocaine is the most rapidly growing cause of AIDS, the drug abuser is not only putting himself or herself at risk of this fatal disease, but also perhaps a spouse, a sex partner, or future children.

Mr. D. was a fifty-five-year-old stockbroker who was seen because he was unable to quit cocaine abuse even after two years of counseling. He said that he was trying to reduce the amounts used because he had become anxious and depressed. When I suggested that he should attempt to stop cocaine completely, he looked at me and pleaded, "What can I use instead?" It was obvious that he had no real intention of quitting drug abuse.

Self-medication with any mind-altering drug can cause fatigue, depression, and intellectual impairment—especially when used on a regular basis. Miss L. was a seventeen-year-old girl typical of a number of young people who were using marijuana almost daily. She complained of inability to remember many routine items, fatigue, and lack of ambition to do things previously enjoyed. This resulted in a marked drop in her scholastic record and in her giving up her desire to become a nurse. In addition, she was noted by her family to have wide variations in mood from depression to inappropriate silliness. After stopping her drug usage for one month, she noted improvement in memory and emotional stability, but still experienced easy fatigue for several more months.

Caffeine Withdrawal

For those who are actually addicted to caffeine, or prone to migraine headaches, a temporary period of headaches for several days to a week may occur in about 10 percent of those who completely stop caffeine. This is not dangerous and will be transient. Others may feel sleepy for about a week while they are adjusting to the lack of artificial stimulation from caffeine. Performing regular exercise will be helpful in these cases. For those with migraine headaches or asthma, gradual reduction of caffeine may help prevent flareups of those disorders.

Physical Benefits

Should everyone follow these four metabolic steps? This depends on the goals of the individual involved. This chapter has been devoted to those with emotional symptoms or fatigue who could benefit from these steps. But what about those who feel that they have no anxiety, hypoglycemia, fatigue, or depression? For these people, the plan may not seem indicated. On the other hand, if good physical health is one of their goals, it might be applicable, especially for specific physical ailments or tendencies.

For example, caffeine restriction is of great benefit for those with a tendency to high blood pressure, heart rhythm disturbances and most forms of indigestion, including heartburn, peptic ulcer, hiatal hernia, irritable colon, and nervous stomach. Regular exercise and the limitation of sweets and carbohydrates are now recognized not only to help maintain normal weight, but are also thought to be useful in retarding arteriosclerosis. The problems created by alcohol or drug excess can constitute a completely separate book. Anyone who has insomnia usually benefits from not having even one cup of tea or coffee, even in the morning.

Mr. G. had felt perfectly well in all other ways when he was advised to avoid the single cup of coffee that he had each morning. He was complaining of not being able to sleep at all on the two nights during the week that he had to work late in the evening. He was unaware of any other problems, and was pleasantly surprised when he experienced normal sleep without medication after stopping the single daily cup of coffee each morning, especially since he had thought only caffeine at night could keep one awake.

Prevention

This does not mean that those with no physical or emotional reasons need to avoid all caffeine. It would seem reasonable to have up to two cups a day if they enjoy it. However, it is well to keep in mind the option to avoid it permanently if they develop any of the problems mentioned. Obviously, some individuals will be unusually sensitive to even small amounts, while others with no problems might tolerate more. In view of the potency of caffeine, it would seem well-advised for anyone not to drink more than two cups a day. For those who find that they cannot totally quit it, restriction to only one cup a day would still be helpful. Don't forget, most cola soft drinks and some non-cola diet drinks contain caffeine, as do many non-prescription pain remedies.

Although we strongly urge everyone who smokes, especially cigarettes, to quit because of smoking's proven physical health hazards, we cannot state that everyone who does so will necessarily feel better emotionally. While many will feel improvement in energy and well-being, others may display symptoms of depression or anxiety for weeks or even months. This is why many physicians and psychologists do not urge their known depressed patients to quit smoking until after their depression has improved.

We suspect that those who cannot quit smoking in spite of overwhelming evidence of its known cancer-, arteriosclerotic- and emphysema-producing properties are actually chemically addicted to the nicotine in tobacco. As in morphine and alcohol addiction, nicotine appears to temporarily relieve some of the symptoms of depression and severe anxiety by its inhibitory chemical effects upon the nervous system, and withdrawal can cause irritability, muscle spasms, restlessness, sleep disturbance and depression. These chemical effects are supported by evidence that smokers have far more side effects and fewer benefits from many medications, including tranquilizers. And, as is true in other addictions, those most predisposed tend to have pre-existing depression and severe anxiety for which temporary relief with such unhealthy drugs as tobacco can lead to addiction.

Fortunately, many other smokers are not addicted and can quit much more easily. We urge those who cannot readily quit on their own to seek out appropriate medical, psychological, and group methods to help them overcome this potentially lethal addiction.

We have always recommended a well-balanced diet adequate in vitamins and minerals and low in fats and sugars for maintaining health and normal weight. This does not contradict supplemental vitamins for those with inadequate diets, under stress of physical illness, or those who just feel better taking them, as long as they avoid potentially toxic amounts of vitamins A or D. Nor does it contradict the use of large megavitamin doses for schizophrenia under appropriate professional supervision. Also, many who use moderate supplemental amounts of vitamin C seem to get fewer colds.

Obvious Benefits

Our success in obtaining the cooperation of people in following these four simple nutritional and exercise steps has been due to the following: First of all, they are informed that the final decision to do so belongs to them alone. If they decide otherwise, they will not be made to feel guilty or embarrassed. This attitude reinforces the importance of their individuality in making decisions regarding their own health. It also reduces the resistance that would result from displaying a dictatorial, rigid, moralistic manner. Another factor in obtaining patients' cooperation is that they are informed that if they cannot personally detect major improvement in their fatigue or emotional status within three to four weeks, then they may feel free to resume their former habits.

In treating hundreds of patients over a number of years, it is difficult to recall anyone who had sincerely tried these four steps who did not feel significantly improved. The ability to get obvious results within a relatively short period of time has been of great value. In these days of innumerable diets and fads, it is necessary for the individual himself to have personal evidence of effectiveness.

In summary, these four simple metabolic steps have been surprisingly beneficial to our patients for the conditions discussed. They could offer benefits to a great many others with similar problems. For those who suffer from clinical depression, persistent fatigue, recurrent or severe anxiety, hypoglycemic symptoms, or other significant psychosomatic symptoms, it is very important to consult a physician to confirm the diagnosis, rule out underlying organic diseases, and initiate appropriate treatment.

There has been no discussion of depression or other conditions in children because the authors' experience is limited to adults and teenagers in the practice of internal medicine. Therefore, others who do deal with children's problems must determine whether any of our recommendations apply.

Some people with anxiety, depression, or fatigue may already be avoiding caffeine, sugars, and alcohol and may be getting regular exercise. Others may need to try only one or two metabolic steps since they may already be doing the others. Many of them have intuitively noted the effects of these steps previously in helping their symptoms, but still have enough residual problems to require seeing a professional or obtaining new psychological insight for themselves.

Obviously, these four steps cannot be a cure-all. But they can help set the stage for making satisfying decisions when the time comes to make appropriate changes.

CHAPTER 3

How to Tell Whether It's Really Depression —or Mostly Anxiety

You may have wondered if you, or someone close to you, might be suffering from depression. Perhaps it's just a case of anxiety, or maybe it's just being overtired and needing a good vacation. Understandably, you might be fearful to discover that it could really be depression. While most of us are not too uncomfortable with the word anxiety, the term *depression* can often be frightening. This is because of misunderstanding about the basic nature of depression, its implications, frequency, and curability.

Common Misunderstandings

To begin with, depression should not be considered as a mental illness; it involves just as many physical causes and symptoms as it does psychological ones. If one must use a label, emotional illness would be appropriate. It is not a form of insanity; there is usually no loss of contact with reality as might be evidenced by delusions or hallucinations. And the vast majority of depressed people are treated by ordinary family physicians and internists, reserving the use of psychiatrists or psychologists for those whose situations require the additional time, expense, and experience of these specialists.

Since one out of every four people who visit their family physician has the disease called depression, all of us can expect to have personal involvement with this condition, if not within ourselves, then with someone close to us. It's not an unusual illness. You may be wondering what good it would do to find out if you might be depressed, since you may believe that nothing could be done about it anyway. This is perhaps the worst misunderstanding of all, since depression has one of the highest cure rates of any disease, and in a reasonable period of time.

In a way, those who have experienced depression share a common bond with many of the greatest minds in history. Those responsible for much of the world's greatest music, art, literature, and creative science have had to cope with depression at some time during their lives. This suggests that the struggle to overcome this illness may give rise to creativeness and wisdom.

It is most difficult to believe that you can get well, when the disease that you suffer from is often characterized by symptoms of deep pessimism and hopelessness. But you can force yourself to try—you've got nothing to lose by trying and when you do recover, you'll realize the power within you, not only to regain your health and happiness, but also to help pass it along to those around you.

The material discussed in this chapter is intended for everyone, not just physicians and psychologists. This is because all of us must deal with the problems generated by anxiety and depression, whether in personal, family, social, or occupational life. From a practical viewpoint, the awareness of anxiety or depression will not only be useful to indicate when to seek professional help for ourselves or loved ones, but will also be valuable when dealing with others who suffer from these conditions.

Jim, a forty-seven-year-old married salesman, had come in for his annual medical checkup. He appeared comfortable and relaxed when he denied any depression during the preceding year. And he volunteered that he actually had improved in any of these tendencies that he had previously coped with in years past. Jim indicated that he was subject only to the amount of anxiety appropriate to the demands of his job. But in response to the routine question regarding any changes in his sleep pattern, he admitted that for three months he had been awakening repeatedly, after only a few hours of sleep, and had been having great difficulty in falling back to sleep. Because of this he was re-questioned, asking specifically if he had suffered any recent disappointments. It was only then that he related, somewhat reluctantly, that his eighteen-year-

old son had not only lied and stolen money from him, but had run away from home, and had not been heard from since. This had happened just before his sleep problem began. Then he was able to volunteer just how much guilt, anger, and resentment this had caused.

Here, the diagnosis and subsequent treatment for his depression was made possible by an approach which allowed for the detection of a hidden group of symptoms when a more overt one was encountered. There are several reasons why depression can be so difficult to recognize, not only by those personally involved, but also by those responsible for its diagnosis and treatment-family physicians, internists, and even, at times, psychiatrists and psychologists.

First of all, confusion often exists between the meanings of the terms *anxiety* and *depression,* especially since these two conditions often occur together. Similar confusion also occurs between the use of the terms *depression* and *sadness.* Secondly, even when someone does suspect that he may be suffering from the disease of depression, he may be reluctant to reveal it because of false beliefs that it is a sign of weakness of character, or a form of insanity. In addition, the situation leading up to it may be a source of great embarrassment. Thirdly, since the psychosomatic symptoms of depression include such nonspecific symptoms as fatigue, sleep disturbance, weight loss, and a wide variety of physical complaints from associated anxiety, it can readily be appreciated how easy it is to confuse depression with other diseases. If someone is already pessimistic from being depressed, he is apt to believe that any psychosomatic symptom is the result of some catastrophic fatal illness.

Depression-Anxiety Symptoms Chart

The following depression-anxiety chart on the next few pages represents a novel organization of classical symptoms of anxiety and depression, It should be of considerable aid in helping you decide whether a person's condition might be depression or anxiety, or both. But it is only an outline chart, and a final diagnosis requires an outside professional. Most family physicians and internists have the experience and objectivity to make this diagnosis, but occasionally it will require the help of a psychiatrist or psychologist. It is extremely important to consult your personal physician, not only for an accurate diagnosis of depression or anxiety, but also to evaluate psychosomatic symptoms and start treatment if necessary. It should be very helpful to bring to professional attention both your positive and your negative responses to this depression-anxiety chart.

Because depression is readily treatable, it is important for you and your physician to have a systematic approach for its diagnosis, especially, as is often the case, if it occurs in an atypical or misleading manner, The following system organizes the symptoms of depression into four major categories. Whenever a suspicious symptom is found in one category, a more thorough inquiry can be made into the others. To establish the diagnosis, it is usually necessary to have at least two of the major categories represented, and also to consider that some of the more serious symptoms within each category carry more weight than others. Furthermore, the duration of symptoms is crucial to the diagnosis. Symptoms must usually persist for at least several weeks before depression can be diagnosed, and in most cases have been present for months before it actually is diagnosed.

These four categories are separated according to their level of communication. The first are conscious symptoms and comprise distressing thoughts, feelings, and attitudes. The second group consists of the social symptoms communicated to relatives, friends, and co-workers that may be more apparent to others than to the depressed person himself. The third and fourth groups both include psychosomatic physical symptoms communicated from the unconscious mind. These are separated into the vegetative group and the anxiety group. Vegetative symptoms disrupt basic life processes to cause sleep impairment, loss of energy, changes in appetite and weight, and sexual dysfunction; while the anxiety group consists of a variety of physical symptoms, usually in conjunction with feelings of fear or anger. Details of these will follow later in the chapter.

This historical quotation vividly describes some of the conscious symptoms of depression along with two of the most characteristic psychosomatic ones.

In my opinion, nothing is worthwhile; everything is futile. Everything is unutterably weary and tiresome. Nothing is truly new. It has all been done or said before. So what does a man get for all his hard work? Days full of sorrow and grief, and restless, bitter nights.

These words, recorded over 2500 years ago, will sound familiar to those of you who have read the Old Testament, and were attributed to King Solomon in the chapter of Ecclesiastes.

Here was a man who supposedly had everything-prestige, wealth, power, and a thousand wives—and he ended up feeling despair, futility, apathy, boredom, disappointment, and loss of meaning or purpose to life. In addition, he experienced two of the most characteristic vegetative psychosomatic symptoms, persistent insomnia and fatigue. Whether or not Solomon really made these statements, this quotation serves as evidence that depression is at least as old as recorded history; that the symptoms are basically unchanged; and, finally, that this disease can occur even in the most powerful and successful people. In fact, it may be no coincidence that this entire chapter of the Bible, devoted almost entirely to the symptoms of depression, was attributed to the king who presided when Israel was at its peak in wealth and power.

Conscious Symptoms

Of the conscious symptoms, sadness is the one most often confused with depression because both are often mistakenly thought to mean the same thing. So it is important to understand their true relationship to each other. Although some degree of sadness is usually present in the disease of depression, other symptoms are necessary for its diagnosis. Medically, depression actually refers to the disease state, while sadness is the feeling of unhappiness that can either be a normal transient response to everyday stress or a major conscious symptom of depression. In the latter case, the sadness is usually exaggerated out of proportion, in duration and severity, to the stress involved, or, at times, no such stress can even be identified. Its duration in depression is usually measured in weeks or months rather than hours or days as in ordinary sadness. Although sadness need not necessarily be severe, it will be associated with other symptoms of depression if that disease is present.

When sadness is not acknowledged, other terms to indicate varying degrees of unhappiness often will be. These include, in order of severity, loss of enthusiasm, boredom, loss or distortion of sense of humor, disappointment, despair, futility, and hopelessness.

In addition to this breakdown of unhappy mood symptoms, another division of the conscious symptoms is the reduction of self-image. This varies from loss of self-confidence and self- esteem to self-rejection and even self-hatred.

The division of impairment in intellectual functioning may be apparent as an inability to concentrate, inattentiveness, impairment of memory, and often frustrating inability to make even minor decisions.

Guilt, anger, and fear are the conscious symptoms that often are responsible for aggravating and perpetuating the depression. For this reason, this group is called the aggravator symptoms. They not only help cause the depression, but they are also produced by it, in a vicious cycle. Usually, guilt, found with depression, is inappropriate, exaggerated and unwarranted, and can often be improved when a professional makes a firm statement to that effect. Like anger, guilt often involves a close family member.

The prolongation and intensity of anger will also be found to be out of proportion once the person has recovered from his depression. Both guilt and anger involve aggression. In the former the object is one's self, while in the latter it is someone else. Often these aggravator symptoms occur together in varying degrees. In addition to its occurrence in depression, fear is commonly associated with the bodily psychosomatic symptoms of anxiety, which may or may not coexist with depression.

The group of symptoms indicating loss of meaning for life include loss of faith or sense of purpose, feelings of emptiness, loneliness, and isolation, and often a loss of sense of importance to loved ones.

Another division within the conscious symptoms involves attitudes toward the depression itself. These increase in intensity from feelings of frustration and entrapment to the desire to run away; then to thoughts of suicide; and occasionally to the actual carrying out of such an act. It is urgent to seek out prompt professional help if such suicidal thoughts do occur. Ideally, it would be beneficial to seek out help before these desperate considerations even occur.

Social Symptoms

The social symptoms of seclusiveness, instability, unfriendliness, hostility, or jealousy are always more apparent to others than to the depressed person himself, and are therefore organized as the second major category following the conscious symptoms.

Bob, a forty-year-old married insurance salesman, had been brooding for several months over feelings of unfulfillment. He had expected to be at least a local agency manager by his fortieth birthday, but now he felt that his life was more than half over and heading for an insignificant end. At first, his wife thought he was just another case of the "turning-forty blues," but after months of putting up with his unexplained outbursts at her and the children, she began to get seriously concerned. Even more disturbing were his long periods of silence and lack of communication. He would just sit in his chair, motionless, pretending to read or watch television, and not even change the flat expression on his face when he was asked a question. Bob wouldn't even offer any reasonable explanation when he quit his job one morning just grumbling how the boss and the other salesmen had finally gotten rid of the office "flunky." By the time another month had passed, his wife told him that either he went for medical help or she'd be forced to leave him. He had ceased to be a husband in any sense of the word—lover, companion or breadwinner.

Bob's case history illustrates some of the common social symptoms of depression. At times these may be the only clues to this illness when the depressed person is reluctant to disclose his conscious or psychosomatic symptoms. It can be useful for the spouse or a family member to accompany the person to the physician's office when one suspects this illness since the source of information is often more apparent to someone other than the involved person himself.

Social symptoms can be organized further as to verbal and nonverbal communication, the various forms of altered social behavior, and the types of groups involved. The three most closely involved group relationships are the family, friends, and work associates, while the common alterations in social behavior are irritability, seclusiveness, and impairment of role function as spouse, parent, friend or co-worker.

While the contents of verbal communication may include pessimistic, morbid, or hostile speech, the manner of speech may be low in volume, slow and hesitant, monotonous in pitch and sparse in amount. Infrequently, a high-pitched, choppy, staccato manner of speaking may be observed in depressed women.

Irritability and hostility are often first felt by the family, and then later may involve friends and co-workers. Gradually, withdrawal from family participation and social activities

Rapid Diagnostic Depression-Anxiety Chart

Categories of Depression Symptoms

I. Conscious Symptoms

A. Degrees of Sadness
1. Boredom
2. Loss of enthusiasm
3. Loss of sense of humor
4. Pessimism
5. Dissatisfaction
6. Disappointment
7. Sadness (unhappiness)
8. Futility
9. Desperation

B. Reduction in Self-Image
1. Loss of self-confidence
2. Loss of self-esteem
3. Self-rejection
4. Self-hatred

C. Aggravator Symptoms
1. Fear—also common in anxiety
2. Anger
3. Guilt

D. Impairment in Intellectual Function
1. Lack of concentration
2. Impairment in attentiveness
3. Impairment of memory
4. Difficulty in making decisions

E. Attitudes toward Problems
1. Frustration
2. Entrapment
3. Desire to run away
4. Unsolvable (helplessness)
5. Hopelessness
6. Suicidal thoughts
7. Suicidal preparations
8. Past history of suicide attempt

F. Loss of Meaning for Life (alienation)
1. Isolation
2. Loneliness
3. Emptiness
4. Feeling of abandonment
5. Loss of sense of importance to others
6. Loss of faith or purpose
7. Loss of meaning for life

II. Social Symptoms

A. Verbal Communication
1. Content of speech
a. Silence
b. Sparse
c. Pessimistic
d. Morbid
e. Hostile
f. Guilt-ridden
2. Manner of Speech
a. Slow
b. Hesitant
c. Monotonous pitch
d. Low volume

B. Nonverbal Communication
1. Personal appearance and grooming
a. Unkempt clothing and hair
b. Abandonment or sloppy use of cosmetics
2. Psychomotor retardation (general slowing down of bodily movement)
3. Depressed body posture
4. Depressed or flat facial expression

C. Changes in Social Behavior
1. Irritability
2. Seclusiveness
3. Impairment of performance of role function (such as husband, occupation, friend)
4. Unfounded jealousy
5. Unfriendliness

For scoring sections I, II, and III, see page 36

Unconcious Psychosomatic Groups When Not Due to
Physical Causes

III. Psychosomatic Vegetative Group
   A. Persistent Early-morning Insomnia or Excessive Need to Sleep
   B. Loss or Gain in Appetite and Weight
   C. Loss of Energy
   D. Sexual Disturbances

IV. Psychosomatic Anxiety Group
   A. Fearfulness, Restlessness, Agitation
   B. Initial Difficulty in Falling Asleep
   C. Anxiety Attacks or Hyperventilation (palpitation, breathlessness, dizziness)
   D. Skeletal Muscle Spasm
      1. Tension headache
      2. Back-of-neck pain
      3. Backache
      4. Chest muscle pain
      5. Extremity muscle spasm

   E. Involuntary Smooth Muscle Spasm
      1. Migraine headache
      2. Gastrointestinal spasm
         a. Esophagus—difficulty in swallowing and chest pain
         b. Stomach—upper abdominal pain, nausea, or vomiting
         c. Colon—lower abdominal pain, diarrhea, constipation
   F. Urinary Tract—frequency and pain
   G. Genital Tract—impotence, frigidity, menstrual irregularity

Conditions Commonly Associated with Depression
But Not Specific for It

A. Obsessions—unreasonable fears
B. Compulsions—inappropriate ritualized habits
C. Alcohol Excess
D. Drug Dependency
E. Recent Divorce or Family Loss
F. Severe Obesity
G. Chronic or Severe Physical Disease
H. Antisocial or Criminal Behavior

Numerical Scoring Code for the Depression Symptoms of The Depression-Anxiety Chart

(30 points or more indicates possible depression*)

I A (1) - 1
   (2) - 2
   (3) - 2
   (4) - 2
   (5) - 3
   (6) - 3
   (7) - 3
   (8) - 4
   (9) - 5
   ___
   25 points

I B (1) - 1
   (2) - 2
   (3) - 3
   (4) - 4
   ___
   10 points

I C (1) - 2
   (2) - 3
   (3) - 4
   ___
   9 points

I D (1) - 1
   (2) - 2
   (3) - 2
   (4) - 3
   ___
   8 points

I E (1) - 2
   (2) - 2
   (3) - 3
   (4) - 4
   (5) - 5
   (6) - 5
   (7) - 5
   (8) - 5
   ___
   31 points

I F (1) - 2
   (2) - 2
   (3) - 2
   (4) - 2
   (5) - 2
   (6) - 3
   (7) - 3
   ___
   16 points

II A (1) - 3
   (2) - 3

II B (1) - 4
   (2) - 4
   (3) - 4
   (4) - 4

II C (1) - 2
   (2) - 3
   (3) - 3
   (4) - 3
   (5) - 3
   ___
   36 points

** III A - 5
        B - 3
        C - 4
        D - 3
        ___
        15 points

Total = 150 points

**Chart is not scored beyond this section.

*With exception of organic brain disorders such as senile dementia or mental retardation.

The numerical scoring code for the depression chart allows for differential weight for different depression symptoms. Since this is assigned on the basis of a simple positive or negative response, it spares one the time and indecision of having to rate any symptom according to varying degrees of severity. The psychosomatic anxiety symptoms in group IV and the conditions commonly associated with depression are not scored since these are only indirectly related. The social symptoms are also completed by the individual but if necessary can be evaluated by the family also. With a maximum rating of 150 points, it is recommended that over 30 points be considered as possible depression, but this requires professional confirmation by a physician or psychologist.

occurs. Impairment in work performance, along with inability to get along with co-workers and supervisors, may lead to loss of employment by quitting, being discharged, or taking sick leave.

Strain may lead the spouse to divorce and alienate other family members. Inappropriate anger and irritability often alternate with silence and isolation. Spontaneity of communication may almost stop, with the only conversation consisting of brief apathetic replies to direct questions, Unfounded jealousy may occur at times. Loss of interest in sex, impotency or frigidity may occur and further aggravate marital strain.

Social life gradually decreases, with loss of enthusiasm and even aversion to going out and being seen by friends. Hobbies, sports, and recreation previously enjoyed often become boring and unimportant.

Nonverbal communication includes changes in personal appearance and becomes evident in more severe degrees of depression. Social apathy may become apparent in disregard for personal grooming, lack of care of the hair, unkempt clothing, and abandonment of the use of previously used cosmetics.

Characteristic positioning and changes in bodily mobility may also occur in severe cases. There is often a general slowing down of all muscular movement, known as psychomotor retardation. Here, the person may sit or lie motionless for long periods, doing little or nothing. When he does walk, it is slow and shuffling. The back may be hunched over, head bowed toward the ground, and the hands may be hidden in the pockets or behind the back.

A flat, immobile, unresponsive facial expression may be seen, with lack of spontaneous smiling and, often, a down-turned month. At times this may be only transient, when the person thinks he is not being observed. A fixed, broad smile may occasionally mask true feelings and betray itself by its constancy. Troubled-appearing eyebrows drawn close together, with vertical furrows above the nose and narrowing of the eye slits, may suggest depression even in the presence of a cover-up smile.

It may appear as if the depressed person has two different personalities. These alternate according to mood changes, and are revealed mainly to close family members, at least initially. As discussed in later chapters, this Jekyll and Hyde change of personalities becomes evident not only as hostile or seclusive behavior, but in actual change of physical appearance and facial expression. This duality in depression explains the frequency of such expressions as "My husband seems like a total stranger to me." While the immediate family is most likely to experience this unfriendly personality, it may become evident to others as the condition progresses.

This tendency toward a dual personality will be especially marked if the depression is associated with alcohol or drug dependency as is often the case.These problems often go unrecognized because of our cultural acceptance of the use of alcohol as a drug to tranquilize our brain. This same unhealthy logic will allow the use of recreational drugs as well.

Psychosomatic Symptoms

Psychosomatic symptoms from the unconscious mind comprise the major categories that are most likely to lead one to consult a physician. These are the symptoms that imitate organic physical diseases and often confuse both patient and physician.

Jane, a thirty-eight-year-old divorced writer, appeared tense and fearful as she related how she had suffered continuous back pain for two years. She felt that this pain was responsible for the constant fatigue which caused her to spend most of the time in bed. Jane admitted that she had had normal X-rays of the spine one and one-half years previously, and had a normal physical examination by both her family physician and an orthopedic specialist. Her voice then dropped and her eyes lowered as she recalled how her physician had told her that it might take several years for "it" to show up on the X-rays. After she was asked what she meant by "it," she at first responded with silence, then reluctantly added, "You know, cancer." Then, on further questioning, she admitted that her physician had never used that word. Finally, she was willing to admit that she might have misunderstood him. She had been too frightened by this possibility to even ask him for clarification. In addition to persistent fatigue and back pain, she had also been experiencing middle-of-the-night awakenings with inability to get back to sleep. In despair, she had already given up any hope of recovery.

After discussing the functional nature of her condition, she began to accept the possibility that it could be the result of anxiety and depression. She was further reassured by a thorough examination, normal repeated spinal X-rays, and a detailed explanation of the psychosomatic physiology that had caused all her symptoms. When seen a month later, she had already noted almost complete improvement in back pain, fatigue, and sleep pattern, and had given up her pain medication.

Psychosomatic symptoms arise from real physical and chemical alterations in function of the organs involved; they are not imaginary. The mechanisms involve muscle spasm, altered secretions from glandular tissues, and changes in the rate or intensity of rhythmic functioning in such organs as heart, lungs, or digestive tract. In addition, changes in circulation are frequently due to temporary dilation or contraction in the diameter of certain blood vessels. Most importantly, all of these changes are not usually associated with permanent structural alterations in anatomy and, as a result, these disturbing symptoms do not ordinarily involve physical threat to survival. Psychosomatic symptoms arise from temporary chemical disruptions in the brain brought on by emotional stresses and are transmitted throughout the autonomic nervous system to any organ in the body.

To complete the four major categories of depression, the psychosomatic is divided into the vegetative group and the anxiety group. Vegetative symptoms involve several disruptions of basic biologic functions such as disturbance in sleep, lack of energy, disturbance in appetite with weight change, and disruption of sexual function.

Vegetative Psychosomatic Symptoms

The most characteristic vegetative symptom is the type of sleep disturbance in which one may fall asleep initially, but awaken for no apparent reason after only several hours of sleep, and have great difficulty falling back to sleep. Usually, the person spends this period of wakefulness worrying and being upset. Since this form of early morning insomnia does not usually occur in just simple anxiety, it is often the most striking clue to the possibility of depression and is present in about 70 percent of those with this illness.

In addition, other forms of sleep disturbances that can occur in either anxiety or depression are insomnia for falling asleep initially, nightmares, and restless sleep. On the other end of the scale are those depressed people who require excessive amounts of sleep. But this latter symptom can occur with any cause of fatigue.

Not only does fatigue tend to be worse in the morning, but so do most of the other symptoms of depression such as sadness, hopelessness, fear, anger, and guilt. Although the reasons for this are not known, we suspect that in part it may be related to disturbed sleep. Daily fluctuations in energy often seem to correlate with the varying intensity of depression, suggesting some common rhythmic brain chemical disturbances.

Chronic persistent fatigue for no apparent reason such as a recent illness or overwork is an even more common vegetative symptom of depression than is the inability to stay asleep. But it is not as specific for depression, since it can also occur as a result of other causes, such as lack of exercise, poor nutrition, overwork, or various illnesses.

Unlike the fatigue in most physical illnesses, functional fatigue from depression is often worse in the morning, on awakening, and improves during the day. Occasionally, it may increase as the day goes on. It is usually described as a lack of energy, enthusiasm, or "get up and go," or a drowsiness, sleepiness, or fuzzy-headedness, rather than an actual muscle weakness.

Loss of appetite with sudden weight loss is the vegetative symptom most likely to prompt the person to see his physician because of fear of some serious organic disease. On the other hand, depression can also lead to increased food intake and may result in severe overweight. Appetite alterations occur in over 50 percent of those with depression.

Disturbance in sexual interest or capacity is not only a conscious or social symptom but is a frequent vegetative symptom, most commonly in the form of persistent impotency or frigidity. When temporary, these are often due to simple anxiety alone. Occasionally, increased sexual activity can result from either anxiety or depression.

Anxiety Symptoms

The anxiety group of symptoms may occur alone or in combination with depression. Since anxiety and depression often occur together, they are often confused with each other. Because some tranquilizers used for anxiety may occasionally worsen an unrecognized depression, it is very important to be aware of their distinguishing characteristics. Conversely, antidepressant medication will often, but not always, relieve any associated anxiety when it accompanies depression.

Anxiety itself is considered a symptom and not an entire disease process as is depression. While the term, *anxiety,* is often loosely used to indicate any transient worry or concern, we define it medically to indicate the combination of such conscious symptoms as fear, anger, or guilt in association with a variety of bodily symptoms. Anxiety does not necessarily indicate the presence of an associated depression, since it occurs most often by itself. But when anxiety is frequent, persistent, unrelieved, and of sufficient intensity to interfere with everyday life, then one should suspect the possibility of underlying depression and search the other categories for symptoms of this disease. In fact, chronic anxiety is, itself, a major cause of depression. Like the visible part of an iceberg, overt anxiety often overshadows the more weighty but hidden underlying depression and may require patient effort for its unveiling.

More often than not, depression is accompanied by anxiety and then it is called anxiety-depression. When depression is not accompanied by anxiety, it is then called apathetic and is more likely to be associated with the general slowing down of movement called psychomotor retardation. This latter form comprises a minority of those with depression and is also called endogenous because, in these cases, there's often no obvious recent stress such as loss of a loved one, major disappointment, or unresolved conflict.

We suspect that the frequent association of anxiety with depression must somehow be related biochemically to the chronic excessive release of epinephrine and norepinephrine that occurs during anxiety. It seems reasonable to theorize that the excess production and utilization of these enzymes over months or years could exhaust the brain's capacity to continue to maintain adequate amounts of similar chemicals for normal mood, energy, and intellectual physiology. Similarly, endogenous depression without anxiety may also have a direct impairment of production of adequate norepinephrine or serotonin in the mood and energy centers of the brain.

Anxiety or panic attacks are those in which agitation and excessive bodily movement occur in association with palpitation, sweating, tremulousness, breathlessness, and often dizziness.

These physical symptoms are usually associated with a feeling of panic or fear, but occasionally with anger or guilt.

Since the individual may understandably fear that he is having a heart attack, he may go directly to an emergency room or to his physician's office. Even when there is no associated chest discomfort due to a chest muscle spasm it is important for him to be evaluated by a physician, at least initially, so he can learn to identify and understand the harmless, though frightening, nature of his problem. When one of the major symptoms of these attacks is the feeling of not being able to get enough air, it is called hyperventilation syndrome, The resulting overbreathing often causes dizziness and numbness or tingling in the extremities.

The intensity of anxiety reactions is often out of proportion to any particular stressful situation and often no immediate stress can even be identified, since the underlying stress may be long-standing and repressed. Many of these symptoms of anxiety attacks can be attributed to excessive secretion of adrenalin. This may help explain why abstaining from caffeine will often be helpful.

The bodily reactions occurring during anxiety attacks can be understood when compared to the "fight or flight" bodily preparations for physical life-threatening emergencies. Here, physical survival by fighting or fleeing would be facilitated by the increased level of blood sugar needed as fuel for additional energy, afforded by the effect of additional adrenalin acting on liver stores of glycogen starch. This greater concentration of fuel is then carried more quickly to the muscles by the adrenalin's increase in the heart rate; and the greater rate and depth in breathing would meet the body's increased emergency demands for more oxygen to burn the glucose and get rid of the greater amount of resulting waste product, carbon dioxide.

Since most of our modern-day conflicts are psychological and sedentary rather than physical, the energy generated from these physiologic preparations cannot be dissipated and results instead in psychosomatic anxiety symptoms. Curiously, many of the symptoms associated with anxiety and depression, such as palpitations, breathlessness, and light-headedness along with loss of appetite and sleep, can be due to joy rather than fear or sadness when they occur as a result of sudden great happiness such as falling in love or winning a much sought-after goal. This suggests some common elements in both joy and depression and may be a factor in those cases of depression that follow material success.

The other groups of anxiety symptoms stem from a wide variety of organ dysfunctions that usually do not occur as abruptly as anxiety attacks, and the conscious awareness of fear or anger may be minimal or repressed. Nevertheless, there is usually some amount of these emotions present when looked for.

Many of these symptoms occur as a result of muscle spasm in any part of the body. Skeletal muscle spasm often focuses at any level in the spine and when not due to injury, virus, or bone changes, can simply be due to emotional tension. Even in the presence of arthritis or degenerated discs, emotional tension may be a trigger to initiate spasm and pain. "You give me a pain in the neck" is a statement apparently based on folk wisdom.

When muscle spasm occurs in the scalp it is called tension headache and is a steady, tight sensation. These common tension headaches may at times be confused with another common form of psychosomatic headache-migraine. In the latter the headache usually has a throbbing quality, is often associated with nausea and, in a minority of cases, is immediately preceded by moving spots in front of the eyes. This headache is due to dilation of scalp arteries, preceded by a spasm. In addition to emotional causes, migraine and tension headaches can also be caused by other factors such as diet, allergy and eyestrain.

When muscle spasm occurs in the chest wall, it may be mistaken for heart pain and can occur in association with anxiety or other causes. It requires a physician's evaluation.

In contrast to skeletal muscle spasm in the superficial voluntary muscles in the body and extremities, smooth muscle spasm occurs in the organs found deep in the chest and abdomen, as well as in the walls of the arteries. When spasm occurs in the digestive tract, the resulting symptoms will depend on the location of the part involved, as well as associated changes in the amount of digestive juices secreted. In the esophagus it could cause chest pain, heartburn, difficulty in swallowing, and regurgitation, while in the stomach it could result in upper abdominal pain or vomiting. In the colon, it is called irritable colon or spastic colitis and causes lower abdominal pain, with either diarrhea or constipation.

In these digestive disturbances, stress factors are often associated with intolerance to spicy, coarse, or rich types of food. It often requires a medical examination, with special X-rays and lab tests, to make sure, initially, that the symptoms are not due to a specific physical disease. Peptic ulcer may be an exception to the definition of psychosomatic problems because it does involve an anatomic erosion in the wall of the stomach or small intestine and yet is considered to be related, at least in part, to stress.

Involvement of the heart and lungs in anxiety has already been discussed under anxiety attacks or hyperventilation syndrome. Coronary heart disease has not been listed as a psychosomatic problem because so many other factors are involved, as well as the anatomic changes that occur.

Urinary tract symptoms may include bladder spasm, discomfort and frequency of urination and will also require professional evaluation to rule out physical causes.

Anxiety, as well as physical disorders, can cause irregularities of the menstrual period, lower abdominal pain, infertility, and, very rarely, false pregnancy. In the male, impotency is the most common genital anxiety or depressive symptom.

Compulsions and Phobias

Another group of symptoms that are not confined to depression but occur also as independent emotional problems are called compulsions. These are inappropriate, ritualized behavior patterns seemingly without purpose. However, they have unconscious symbolic meaning to the person involved and temporarily relieve anxiety. Examples are unnecessary, repeated hand washing or touching things in a certain order. Obsessive phobias are unreasonable fears that prevent a variety of normal, everyday activities. These include agoraphobia (fears of open or closed places), fear of crowds, or fear of certain methods of transportation.

Agoraphobia is a term originally used to describe fear of open places but it includes other situations as well. The condition often makes it difficult for the afflicted person to leave his home without experiencing a panic, or anxiety, attack.

Manic-Depressive Illness

Manic-depressive illness, or bipolar depression, is a less frequent form of depression that often alternates with periods of hyperactive false euphoria. Usually these different phases persist for months, and are often separated by normal periods. In many, there will be only the manic or the depressive episodes. This form of depression might be suspected by family history, or by the patient's response to lithium medication.

The manic phase is evidenced by overactivity, quickly changing thoughts and speech, false sense of well-being, and overconfidence. Often poor judgment will be evident by over-spending, unwise investments and at times bizarre behavior. Frequently the overactivity will prevent adequate amounts of sleep.

Although there seems to be a genetic biochemical cause for manic-depressive illness, only a small minority of family members will ever develop it. A therapeutic hallmark of this illness is that continuous long-term treatment with lithium carbonate medication will usually prevent recurrences of both the manic and depressive phases of this illness. However, it is not usually effective for most other forms of depression, often requires other medication to treat the depression initially, and can be monitored for safe effective serum levels by regular blood tests.

At times, it may be difficult for even a professional to differentiate an early stage of depression from a limited case of the "blues," which will subside in a few days to a week or so. Here, the combination of anxiety with sadness or disappointment may even be associated with such psychosomatic symptoms as initial or early morning insomnia, fatigue, or weight loss. For all practical purposes, this does represent a limited or mild case of depression, and as long as it clears up completely within a week or so, no treatment may be needed. Some physicians might properly prescribe a temporary tranquilizer for a few days if the anxiety is severe, and we have found the metabolic recommendations often to be helpful. Usually there is an obvious disappointment, loss, conflict or stress that can be identified. Should the depression symptoms persist for over two weeks, however, then it can be treated as a full clinical depression.

Some people may have a form of cyclic recurring depression for several weeks, alternating with several weeks of improvement, and respond also to treatment for depression. Similarly, when premenstrual depressive symptoms are so severe that a woman is prevented from carrying out her usual responsibilities for several days a month, there is often at least an underlying milder depression that can be treated. However, the most common form of premenstrual tension combines irritability with only limited amounts of sadness, which completely subside without treatment in a few days. These are called the *premenstrual syndrome*.

Another condition that might be confused with the disease of depression is what could be called the chronic pessimistic personality. But there are usually no major psychosomatic symptoms or social symptoms of depression, and the conscious symptoms are usually limited to milder degrees of sadness and disappointment with absence of deep despair and suicidal thoughts, and little if any guilt or anger. These individuals often maintain variable amounts of fear, especially regarding health and aging. Since these pessimistic attitudes are deeply ingrained in the character of the individual, drug therapy is often not helpful or indicated. Psychotherapy, if desired, might offer insight and at least some improvement in the degree of pessimism and sadness.

Schizophrenia

Schizophrenia is an uncommon illness readily differentiated from depression by the occurence in schizophrenia of inappropriateness in some of the following categories: (1) bizarre intellect—sufficiently strange false beliefs and thinking to be considered delusions; (2) bizarre perception—experiencing sensations, usually by seeing or hearing what is not apparent to any others (hallucination); (3) inappropriate mood to the situation—reacting with happiness to sad situations and vice versa, or inability to feel any emotion; (4) bizarre behavior of sufficient degree to be considered beyond the reasonable limits of so-called sanity.

When depressive mood accompanies or alternates with schizophrenic symptoms, this condition may be called a schizo-affective disorder. In this situation it is usually considered as a form of schizophrenia and not depression, in both origins and treatment.

Schizophrenia has been found to be more physical or organic than once thought. Alterations of brain symmetry and atrophy have been found in some cases, using cat scan X-rays, MRI, and research instruments, called PET scanners (positron emitters). Such instruments have disclosed brain areas with abnormal patterns of blood glucose metabolism.

Genetic aspects have long been suspected, and new research in DNA genetic technology is promising. Chemically, it is known that some individuals tend to manufacture excessive amounts of a brain chemical, dopamine, within the brain. This is why most medications developed for this disease aim to reduce the amount of brain dopamine—and still newer medications for schizophrenia are being developed. The complexities of this condition require the skills of a psychiatrist.

Frequent Associations

The following situations have a very frequent association with depression: alcoholism, drug dependency, recent divorce, severe obesity, chronic disabling or life-threatening physical diseases, and chronic antisocial behavior in crime or delinquency. These will be discussed in later chapters.

Why should this chapter be of interest if you have decided that you are not depressed? First of all, you might gain insight which would help to prevent its occurrence in the future. Secondly, it may help in understanding those with depression among your family, friends, and co-workers. Finally, developing a way of living that would help control anxiety and prevent depression should allow a greater amount and longer duration of happiness. Realizing your potential for enjoying what you already have, learning how to make healthy, satisfying decisions, and being aware of simple nutritional factors to help prevent anxiety and depression can improve your quality of life, no matter what mood level you usually have.

The Depression-Anxiety Chart should help to recall and summarize the symptoms of depression. But since the Chart can only suggest its possibility, it is extremely important to consult a physician, psychiatrist, or psychologist to confirm or refute its diagnosis and to initiate any appropriate treatment. Similarly, it is advisable not to assume the responsibilities of a professional when you suspect depression in someone else. Here the appropriate response would be to encourage that person to consult a physician or counselor, if there were reason to believe that the suggestion might be appreciated.

Any symptoms identified from the Chart or otherwise should be brought to the attention of the professional, since almost any symptom could result from this illness. Underlying these symptoms is a chemical imbalance in the brain's mood center. Here deficiency in the neurotransmitters norepinepherine and serotonin are thought to be responsible for the diffuse physiologic and psychologic disturbances. There-

fore, the disease of depression is as physical as it is psychological.

CHAPTER 4

What to Do If You Think It's Depression or Severe Anxiety

Overcoming the powerful disruption that is depression is the major purpose for this book. Its personalized approach was born of the practical necessity to provide help so that those with this disease could help themselves. However, an appropriately skilled human being would be far more therapeutic than any book could possibly be to help one overcome this problem. No book, lecturer, organization, or media presentation could possibly offer the continuing individualized feedback and two-way communication found in the traditional doctor-patient relationship. Variations of this therapeutic partnership include the use of psychologists, psychiatrists, clergymen, and other experienced counselors.

Partnership Approach

This partnership approach between physician (or counselor) and patient will promote the best possible climate for promptly regaining health—not only for depression, but for any illness. First of all, it reaffirms that the patient and physician (or therapist) are both equally important human beings, and refutes the unhealthy bias, maintained by a minority of patients and professionals, that a patient is someone subservient to the expertise of a superior titled professional. This latter distortion is not only harmful to the patient, but is equally harmful to the mental health of those professionals who would pretend to be other than mortal human beings. Therefore, a partnership emphasizes the importance of the patient's individuality, and will begin to elevate his lowered self-image even on the first visit. It will, furthermore, relieve the anxiety of the patient that the physician or therapist might pass judgment on his attitudes or behavior. This security and reassurance will encourage the kind of cooperation necessary on the part of the patient and avoid the withholding of vital but potentially embarrassing information.

The success of any treatment depends in large part on its acceptability to the patients. They have every right to be treated as unique individuals and have their feelings and attitudes respected. The therapeutic power of any medications will be greatly influenced by the attitudes of those who must swallow them. And the patients' readiness to volunteer feedback on the effectiveness of treatment, or their willingness to tolerate transient side effects will depend on the openness and mutual respect of the relationship. This attitude still recognizes the responsibility of the physician to make his professional recommendations, as strongly as he feels indicated, based on his past training and experience.

Consulting a Physician

For a number of reasons, the family physician, internist, or pediatrician is in the best position to be of help, at least initially, for the diagnosis and subsequent treatment of depression. They would also be the ones to treat the anxiety and psychosomatic symptoms that usually accompany depression, and they are crucial to rule out and treat other diseases that could cause depression or simulate it.

For example, it is not unusual to see depression due to lack of adequate thyroid production (hypothyroidism) clear up completely within several weeks of taking thyroid medication. Similarly, estrogen replacement therapy may cure some but not all cases of depression that occur shortly after the onset of menopause, especially if the cessation of menstrual periods is associated with other menopausal symptoms such as hot flashes, headache, and insomnia. The only way to find out if many of the menopausal depressions will respond to estrogen hormone treatment is to try it, providing there are no medical contraindications. Any endocrine glandular disorder can cause emotional changes.

In fact, almost any disease can precipitate depression, including such diverse examples as heart failure, cerebral arteriosclerosis, kidney failure, chronic hepatitis, infectious mononucleosis or any chronic disorder. Consulting a personal or family physician is very important to rule out organic diseases that occasionally cause depression.

Since the majority of those with depression do not necessarily have other diseases, a very important function that a physician might fulfill would be to identify and point out any of a wide variety of naturally occurring and artificial drugs that have the capacity to cause or aggravate depression.

Finding the Right Physician

If you do not already have a family physician or internist, or one with whom you feel comfortable, how might you obtain the services of one who could be appropriate to your needs? This is not always an easy quest. First, physicians are, after all, human beings whose variation in personality, mood, communication skills, and compassion vary as in the rest of the population. Furthermore, their interest and skills in treating emotional problems will often depend on the personality traits mentioned above. Nevertheless, if you don't wait until the last minute for a crisis to occur, you should be able to find a physician suitable for your needs.

Keeping in mind the importance of both technical competency and intuitive understanding, one could inquire of friends, other professionals such as specialists, pharmacists, nurses, and dentists, as well as by phone with the prospective physicians' receptionists, as to whether or not a prospective physician is interested in dealing with those who might have emotional problems. Questions could be asked such as, "Does he have, or will he allow, the time needed for a thorough history and examination?", "Does he seem to like people as people, or is he concerned only with their diseases?", and "Does he explain and encourage the patient to ask questions, or does he seem to function mainly by giving orders and expecting unquestioning obedience?"

Once you have obtained some leads from these sources, you have two choices, either of which could be satisfactory. One would be to set up an appointment for a complete history and physical examination, and the other would be to make a briefer appointment for just an office visit. The advantage of the former is that you could accomplish what will ultimately be needed on the initial contact. It might take longer for this thorough an exam, and if you and the physician were not comfortable with each other, you'd be out a larger amount of money. On the other hand, if the recommendations came from usually reliable sources, it would be unlikely not to be a good match, unless you're very difficult to satisfy. Making a brief appointment just to meet and evaluate a prospective physician takes more courage than most people have. For practical purposes, it might be less awkward for most new patients to have a conventional medical purpose for the office visit, such as a blood pressure check or to check out any symptom present. This would actually allow better evaluation of the physician's usual thoroughness and personal concern than if he thought he was just being critically evaluated.

Your life could some day depend on which physician you choose. When you select a general physician, you not only select him, but usually the whole team of specialists whom he will recommend if and when you need them. This is extremely important, since those specialists that the physician recommends will usually reflect his own attitudes of competency, honesty, and compassion.

Evaluating Media Information

An increasingly important necessity that only the family physician or internist can supply is one that was not even necessary until the past fifteen years or so. This is the combination of technical experience and common sense needed to evaluate all the frightening and confusing articles about medical problems that appear daily in the news media. These stories are often based on preliminary, unproven data and have often caused unnecessary anxiety regarding all the food we eat, the water we drink, and all appropriately prescribed medications.

The family physician or internist is in a position to diagnose and treat not only depression, but other possible associated diseases. He can also prescribe antidepressant medication, offer common sense supportive psychotherapy, and uncover any of a wide variety of natural or artificial drug aggravators of the depression. Not least important is his professional awareness of which psychiatrists and psychologists may be the most skilled and appropriate to your individual needs if it becomes apparent that you should require one of them.

Referral to an Emotional Specialist

The factors that might influence whether or not you might be referred to one of these specialists depend both on your physician's attitudes and your own. These include the confidence, experience, and interest of the general physician in treating depression (or anxiety); the availability of these specialists in the community; the willingness and financial ability of the patient to consult with one (many communities now have inexpensive mental health clinics); the severity and duration of the depression or its response to treatment by the general physician; and if there seems to be a possibility of suicide.

Psychiatrist or Psychologist

The difference between a psychiatrist's and a psychologist's training is probably not as important as are individual differences in human compassion, understanding, and communication skills. However, the psychiatrist has a medical degree, so he can prescribe medication. The psychologist most often has a Ph.D. degree, so he or she has years of training in human behavior, and he might rely on the family physician to prescribe antidepressant medication. In an urgent emotional crisis, it might be necessary to go directly to a psychiatrist or psychologist if you don't have a family physician or if time doesn't allow for his participation. These specialists have the training and skills to provide insights into your psychological problems by going into greater detail in your private personal life. That this may be of great benefit to many does not, in our opinion, mean that it will be necessary for all.

Since it is almost impossible to force someone to see a psychiatric or psychological specialist against his or her will, it may require a reasonable trial of treatment first by the family or general physician before the person can be persuaded that it may be necessary. Nevertheless, there are infrequent circumstances that require forced hospitalization or treatment such as imminent threat of suicide or other self-harming behavior, schizophrenic, alcohol or drug-induced delusions and hallucinations, as well as dangerous personal or antisocial behavior. Just as a minor child would not be allowed by his parents or guardians to not receive medical attention for significant physical symptoms, so it should be for serious emotional symptoms detected in children.

Eliminating Depressing Drugs

Of all the functions that a general physician can provide, none is more important to overcoming or preventing depression and anxiety than the identification and elimination of harmful drug factors. These include not only side effects from appropriately prescribed medications, but also nonprescription drugs; drugs occurring naturally in common foods and drinks, especially beverages such as coffee, tea, and alcohol; legally obtained drugs taken for their chemical effect on the brain; and legal drugs taken in excessive amounts for inappropriate purposes. As more personal experience accumulates in treating depression, it has become evident that these drug factors are the most common readily reversible causes and aggravators of depression. They are also the most overlooked factors by both patient and physician. This is because of the cultural acceptance of drug usage that has conditioned us to accept it as normal in such a drug-dependent society as ours. Especially overlooked have been the factors that were discussed earlier, particularly caffeine and alcohol. It is not routinely recognized that only small amounts of these chemicals could help cause or aggravate depression and anxiety and that these conditions could be helped by their elimination.

A physician requires considerable patience, drug awareness, and compassionate communication skills to uncover how much and what kinds of drugs a patient may be using. It will require even more patience, wisdom, and communication skills to try to convince a drug-dependent patient to suffer the temporary withdrawal discomforts of foregoing these drugs in order to achieve long-term health benefits. The greatest obstacle to this achievement is the drug-impaired brain that cannot adequately think intellectually nor use intuitive common sense to help itself. This is why alcohol and other related drug problems are benefited not only by consulting a physician, psychiatrist, or psychologist, but also require the invaluable support of participating in Alcoholics Anonymous or a drug abuse therapy group. It is unusual to have drug or alcohol dependency without an associated depression. It is difficult to cure depression until the drug problem has been first overcome. A later chapter deals in more detail with alcohol problems.

Any drug capable of causing alterations in mental awareness is capable of causing long-term impairment of brain function. This includes memory loss, impaired judgment for making healthy decisions, mood fluctuations from depression to false euphoria, hallucinations, and loss of ability to initiate and maintain goal-oriented behavior. This is repeatedly observed not only among abusers of alcohol, sedatives, sleeping pills, narcotics, diet pills, stimulants, and LSD, but also in a number of those who used marijuana on a frequent and heavy basis.

What about the depression that occurs as a result of side effects from properly prescribed doses of medication taken for a variety of medical reasons? These are often the most overlooked and difficult to evaluate for both physician and patient.

One should not misconstrue this discussion as a tirade against the use of medication. Proper use of medication has allowed not only a significant prolongation of life but, equally important, a great improvement in the quality of life. All that is required when a depression is recognized is for both the patient and the physician to ask if it is even remotely possible that some medication or other drug factor could be a contributor. Then this possibility could be checked in the Physicians Desk Reference (PDR) to see if depression has ever been reported as a side effect with the particular drugs being used. If so, several alternatives are available that depend on the judgment of the physician, with the cooperation of the patient. One would be to stop the medication for several or more weeks, if it would be safe to do so. Other medications could possibly be substituted at least temporarily, until it is apparent whether or not the original medication was at fault.

Depression can occur as a side effect of birth control pills and high blood pressure medication, but it is less common than that which can occur as a result of the use of some tranquilizers, sleeping pills, appetite suppressants, and stimulants. Yet most of these medications can be of value and one should never stop any medication without prior consultation with one's physician. Rarely, a patient and physician might differ on whether a particular medication might be causing a depression. If the physician were not willing to consider this possibility, a reasonable recourse would be to consult another physician.

The occasional depressing effects of some tranquilizers for those whose anxiety is more apparent than their depression have already been discussed in the previous chapter.

The aggravating effects of caffeine, alcohol, and sugars have been discussed. It is important to emphasize that as the depression or anxiety worsens, more and more aggravating drugs will often be used to temporarily numb the effects of these worsening conditions. These will include not only caffeine, alcohol, and sugars, but also illegal drugs and heavier amounts of sleeping pills and tranquilizers. This vicious cycle must be recognized and interrupted in order to help the person to get well.

Antidepressant Medications

After all this discussion about the potential of many kinds of drugs to cause depression, it may come as a surprise to read here that the greatest advancement for the treatment of depression is the availability of effective antidepressant medication. This does not obviate the need to stop any aggravating drugs before antidepressants can be expected to be fully effective. The use of common-sense supportive psychotherapy by the general physician, along with these chemical measures, makes a practical combination that has been very effective with the vast majority of hundreds of such patients. More detailed psychotherapy is available from specialists when, as discussed earlier, it is required.

The tricyclic antidepression group of medications have been the most effective and safest, along with other types that have recently become available. These work by helping the body to correct deficiencies of two nerve transmitters called serotonin and norepinephrine in certain parts of the brain. Since the medications have no direct effect of stimulation, it may take several weeks to achieve their benefit, but for the same reason they have not led to drug abuse or addiction. Other medications include monamine oxidase inhibitors, phenothiazines having both tranquilizer and antidepressant properties, and lithium carbonate, primarily for manic-depressive illness. In addition, combinations of tranquilizer with antidepressant are occasionally necessary. Most importantly, the choice of appropriate and safest medication must involve an individualized evaluation by the family physician, internist, or psychiatrist.

For those who oppose medication, the avoidance of the aggravating drugs and the obtaining of psychotherapy may at times be effective by itself, but if improvement is inadequate, one should reconsider antidepressant medication. As mentioned earlier, the use of regular exercise will be helpful whether or not medication is taken.

Since insomnia from depression is a common factor for overusing sleeping pills and alcohol, the anti-insomnia effects of antidepressants will often be of benefit. The temporary drowsiness from some of these medications can be minimized by starting with small doses, and taking the entire dosage before bedtime. Smaller doses have often been effective by avoiding alcohol, caffeine, and sugars and getting regular exercise. Increasing the dose may be necessary to obtain good results. Occasionally, the use of a single tablet of a mild sleeping pill or a tranquilizer will be needed with the antidepressant. When possible, the simpler the variety of mind-affecting medications, the less likely there are to be side effects. Lithium drugs have been used mainly for the prevention and treatment of the manic-depressive disease.

Suicide

No discussion of depression would be complete without an evaluation of suicide. Ordinarily, most books would discuss its frequency, age, and sex preferences, and its markedly increased frequency in those with alcohol and drug dependency. It is important to have an approach that is individually oriented. A totally committed, individualistic approach has been a vital factor in helping patients with depression.

Whenever a depressed person presents himself for evaluation and treatment, it is important to inquire about the possibility of suicide, even though the great majority of depressed persons do not actually attempt it. Nevertheless, suicide, usually as a result of depression, is one of the most frequent causes of death in young people, and has been increasing in past years. Many depressed people will at some time entertain vague thoughts about the remote possibility of committing suicide without making serious plans to do so. A smaller number will mentally plan how they might do so. A still smaller number will carry out preparations such as purchasing a gun or saving up pills. Obviously, as one proceeds from vague considerations to mental planning and then carrying out preparations, there is a progressively greater threat that suicide might actually be attempted. Also, a history of a suicide attempt increases that possibility. Anyone who is depressed or who even harbors vague considerations of suicide should be urged to seek professional help promptly.

Since most of those who consider the possibility of suicide would be willing to discuss it, it is very important that the physician or a family member ask directly of any depressed person whether he or she has been considering suicide, and, if so, to what degree of preparation has he gone? It is generally accepted that merely asking about suicide will not increase its likelihood, but could decrease it by stimulating prompt treatment for the underlying depression. Similar to depression's Jekyll and Hyde duality, part of the person may want to commit suicide and the other may be searching for help in avoiding it. Since suicidal thoughts usually are not volunteered, a direct question needs to be asked. Even if such thoughts are denied there is usually no embarrassment.

Once a person acknowledges thoughts about suicide, even though he might deny being depressed, it is very important for him to see a physician, psychiatrist, or psychologist promptly. Especially if the individual seems to have definite plans or intentions for suicide, the professional may recommend prompt hospitalization for treatment. Usually this could not be forced and would have to be done voluntarily. Many communities now have psychiatric facilities as part of a community general hospital, so it is not usually necessary for hospitalization to be carried out in a distant state psychiatric hospital.

What could you say to someone who had just told you that he or she is considering suicide? For those without experience in facing this situation, it could generate a great deal of anxiety, especially for a family member. But it is important to allow discussion about it and to obtain professional help. It may seem a difficult task to refute the false logic of a suicidal solution to a problem that seems insolvable and is accompanied by depression's futility, hopelessness, guilt, self-rejection, and isolation. A professional with previous experience and emotional objectivity is required not only to relieve some of the tension by talking about the problem, but also to point out that the apparent logic of a suicidal solution is based on false assumptions. First of all, depression is not a hopeless disease; it is almost always curable. Secondly, its symptoms of guilt, self-rejection, sadness, and all the others, including psychosomatic symptoms, will disappear once the depression is treated. Even the seemingly insolvable life situation may resolve itself once the depression has been overcome, or its toleration may become possible, or alternatives may be realized that were not previously considered possible during the depression. Usually the use of antidepressant medication and supportive psychotherapy will hasten the disappearance of these suicidal feelings.

Another strong argument against suicide is the emotional harm, guilt, and depression that it usually causes in the surviving members of the family, no matter how undeserved. They always will wonder what they could or could not have done to prevent it.

Finally, even for those without any family or religious beliefs against suicide, the ultimate rejection of one's individuality is to kill one's self. Very few people who consider suicide would seriously consider murder, but in reality they are similar. The taking of a human life is the taking of a human life, no matter whether it is one's own or someone else's. You don't own your life like your own suit of clothes. But you do have a responsibility to respect your individuality and, no matter how tough the going gets, to stick it out and get appropriate help. During many years of experience with hundreds of depressed people, it has been rare to find someone with depression who didn't get well—and get over his suicidal feelings—if he or she accepted the opportunity.

One controversial psychiatrist claims that the right of an individual to commit suicide should not be interfered with. Moderation would indicate, however, that it is an affront to the importance of individuality to destroy it by violence, and humanitarian considerations would confirm the importance of salvaging a human being from infirmity or death when the underlying disease, such as depression, is curable. It might be different if the individual contemplating suicide were in the terminal stages of an incurably fatal disease.

A source of gratification has been the thanks received for treating patients after a suicide attempt who subsequently recover from their depression. Of course, there are those individuals whose suicidal tendencies are the result of more than depression alone; these include those with bizarre delusions as part of schizophrenia and those with alcohol or drug-dependency problems. As long as one persists in impairing the healthy functions of the brain by such chemical poisoning, it's much more difficult to achieve a cure. The incidence of suicide among alcohol and drug abusers is considerably greater than among depressed individuals without these problems. It is vital that those with drug and alcohol problems get the help needed. It's almost as if these individuals were already committing a slow form of suicide. The rapid rise in suicide among young people followed a period of the greatest incidence of drug abuse by young people ever recorded.

Electroshock Therapy

The subject of forcing someone to undergo particular forms of treatment that may seem repugnant to many is an appropriate place to discuss electroshock therapy. There seems to be an intuitive rejection to the use of electroshock therapy by many people, even many professionals. The idea of shocking the brain to make it better seems gross and crude. The temporary memory disturbances also seem frightening, and its use has been associated in the past with being forced to undergo it. The brief treatment is not painful, however, and in recent years medication and the use of anesthesia prevent convulsions.

While the use of electroshock therapy seems unnecessary for the vast majority of those suffering from depression, for those patients who do not respond to any other form of therapy electroshock therapy can often offer prompt, safe, and total recovery, Nevertheless, if the patient or the family should have any misgivings concerning its use, they should feel free to ask for a second psychiatric consultation. In fact, most states require additional consultation.

Causes of Depression

While there is no known single cause for depression, many factors that lead to its occurrence are beginning to be appreciated. These include many physical, psychological, and biochemical factors discussed in this book. Undoubtedly, the greatest future advances will be in further understanding of the relation of brain and body biochemistry to emotions.

The most widely accepted current explanation for the biochemical changes associated with depression is an acquired reduction in the amounts of chemical neurotransmitter in certain mood centers in the brain. These so-called biogenic amines include norepinephrine, serotonin and dopamine, and are chemically responsible for effective electrical nerve conduction from one nerve fiber to another. It is thought that any form of effective treatment will help correct this chemical imbalance, whether through drugs, psychotherapy, electroshock, or even spontaneous recovery. Any factor that can precipitate depression, whether it be psychological, physical or chemically related, is thought to do so by causing this same biochemical change in brain physiology.

The Mood Thermostat

We have devised the concept that a mood thermostat may be discovered someday to actually exist in the brain. We call it the "moodostat." This is a mood thermostat that is evidenced by the tendency of different individuals to display a characteristic level of happiness or sadness when basic life conditions are stable. This is one of the strongest of all the personality traits and terms such as moody, good-natured, optimistic, or pessimistic can often be traced back to infancy and childhood. This suggests a possible hereditary influence and may often explain marked differences in temperament among siblings in the same family.

This relative consistency requires some kind of controlling mechanism such as that seen for appetite, sex, and blood pressure. Like these, it may actually exist in the brain stem. Even if it is never proven, it is a useful concept to remember—that any physical or psychological factor can influence our mood. These influences may temporarily shift the moodostat toward more sadness or happiness and then return to the basic mood after the influence has passed.

Common examples of how a physical factor can influence the mood are weather and climate. Many people feel sad after several days of bad weather. Polar climates are associated with high suicide rates. We speak of a "sunny" disposition or a "stormy" personality. We have all felt sad for several weeks after recovering from the flu or after a surgical operation.

Now you can apply this concept to every factor discussed in this book: chemical factors such as alcohol, sugar, and caffeine; psychological factors such as disappointment, striving for achievement, family conflict, overwork, etc.; and environmental factors such as season, weather, light and darkness, and temperature and humidity. You could undoubtedly add many factors of your own.

Obviously, we could not discuss every aspect of the treatment of depression, both because of limitation of time as well as personal experience. There are many other books that offer statistics and technical data not gone into in our personalized approach.

We have emphasized those aspects of the treatment for depression that we have found not only to be the most effective, but also to be the factors that the average person could do something about. You don't have to be a professional to learn how to find an appropriate physician or specialist, to suspect and eliminate naturally occurring and artificial mind-altering drugs, or to discuss the possibility of a prescribed drug's side effect with your physician. Nor do you need to be a professional to have the compassion and understanding to listen to someone discuss his suicidal thoughts and then encourage him to seek help.

If you happen to be a professional, physician, psychiatrist, or psychologist, you already are aware of the tremendous responsibility that involves working with those who have emotional problems. You are also aware that compassion, intuitive wisdom, importance of individuality, and the partnership approach to the doctor-patient relationship are subjects not taught in college. You certainly have every right to disagree with these concepts, but hopefully you will maintain a high index of suspicion about any potential drug factor that could be important for your patients. Of equally great importance for those of you who take on this responsibility is to emphasize to the patient that he is going to get better; that he is not losing his sanity; and that he is no less an important individual human being for having this illness. In addition, it can be very helpful to see to it that any patient who might profit from antidepressant medication gets the opportunity to use it if he is willing.

CHAPTER 5

Avoiding the Overload Syndrome

A thirty-year-old, formerly enthusiastic young mother developed despondency, insomnia, and episodes of crying a month after undertaking the chairmanship of the local PTA. She had already had a very busy schedule with four volunteer organizations and a full household of responsibilities. After she was encouraged by her physician to drop several of her volunteer jobs, she completely recovered from her symptoms in only a few weeks.

After a usually optimistic fifty-year-old college professor had been promoted to associate dean, he was complimented for his efficiency and was asked by the dean to assume additional responsibilities for someone going on sabbatical leave. Within two months, as he became aware of the lack of time to perform all of these duties, he developed insomnia, anxiety, depression, and chest pain. After a normal physical exam and electrocardiogram he was urged to tell his superior that because of health he would no longer be responsible for the additional tasks. It required only a week to resume his normal state of health.

A young, previously happy receptionist in a psychiatrist's office gradually developed depression, with insomnia, crying spells, and fear of going to work. After a discussion with her employer, she agreed to leave her job and recovered in just a few weeks. In her case, it was not so much the quantity of work that was involved, but rather the content of communication of the patients' anxieties and depressions.

Overload Syndrome

The "overload syndrome" is a temporary anxiety and depression state that results from becoming overburdened with too many work, household, volunteer, or social obligations, and subsides promptly after reducing the excessive responsibilities. Outside pressure to accept these responsibilities is usually a major factor, although many seem eager to take on the extra tasks initially. It can best be likened to overloading an electrical outlet and blowing a fuse. The excessive obligations can either be distributed in a variety of different activities, or in too many responsibilities within a single job. This situation is becoming more frequent due to an increasingly busier way of life, and most of us experience it sooner or later. Usually, it is the hardworking, previously optimistic people who are most prone to this condition. They are the ones who are most often sought to take on additional responsibilities, not only because of their efficiency, but also because of their pleasant nature, which makes them less likely to refuse. The resulting anxiety and depression seems unusual for them, since they had been previously happy. Pessimists may also develop this condition. Common examples include homemakers who join too many volunteer organizations without realizing how much time will really be required, workers simply taking on too many different tasks within their job, or a combination of both. At the time the additional responsibilities are offered, the person either anticipates that they can be easily handled, or he or she may feel pressured to accept them and would be embarrassed to refuse. Since these tasks are usually offered with the assurance that they should take only a minimum of time and effort, it is even more embarrassing when one has to quit because they are endangering his or her health. Anxiety develops not only for fear of not being able to complete all the different tasks, but also because of not being able to accomplish them at one's usually high standards. As anxiety grows, with increasing feelings of entrapment, depression sets in, with its sense of hopelessness and guilt. Irritability and moodiness often disrupt the family's communication. Fatigue, inability to make decisions, and loss of efficiency often develop from the resulting anxiety-depression and further aggravate the situation. Prior recreational and exercise outlets are discarded from apathy and lack of time. Insomnia, especially awakening in the middle of the night and worrying about the incompleted tasks, may leave them exhausted the next morning.

Eventually, many of these people will be willing to drop some of their excess tasks, often only after the situation becomes desperate. Since some may be dropping the overload activities on the advice of their physicians, they avoid the stigma of being a quitter. Since most have not been previously depressed, they will not usually require specialized counseling. Often they improve simply by dropping the excess amounts of obligation. Others who don't recover promptly may require counseling.

Learning to Say "No"

The ideal management of the overload syndrome is to prevent it from occurring in the first place. This can be accomplished by being aware of this condition and avoiding excessive obligations. First, one needs to learn when to say "no!" This does not usually mean rejecting responsibilities already agreed upon beforehand unless it is a matter of health. An example is the duty of a physician to respond to his patients when they become ill, but referring someone not yet his patient to another physician when there isn't enough time to do an adequate job. When someone is called to take on a volunteer position for a worthy organization, many assume "you just can't say no." All it takes is an awareness of one's priorities, then it becomes easier to refuse when it means preserving time and energy for the higher priority of obligations to one's family and health. This does not mean that you need to avoid additional challenges when they are of interest and can be managed adequately.

One must still be prepared, however, to accept some temporary feelings of guilt when refusing requests. It can be embarrassing to say "no" to a job supervisor or a friend who is a volunteer committee chairperson when they ask you to take on important responsibilities. If you are already overloaded, you need a specific plan of relief; whoever is seeking your help will usually ignore anything short of a firm refusal.

Once you recognize that you are suffering from an overload anxiety or depression, you could recover more promptly by enlisting the aid of your physician. Not only would this help to diagnose the cause, but it would also allow treatment of the symptoms and establish an acceptable reason to quit.

Overemphasis on Occupational Identification

Since our society identifies an individual primarily by his or her occupation, it is bound to place a disproportionate emphasis on the importance of that role. The resulting imbalance tends to minimize the necessity for time to spend with family and for recreation. Equating one's job with his or her total individuality has resulted in such obviously biased statements as, "She is just a housewife, while he is an accomplished lawyer." Overemphasis on occupation is so culturally ingrained that it is rarely challenged and causes frequent distortion of self-esteem and self-identity. As a result, occupational stresses are second in importance only to family influences in predisposing to depression and anxiety.

While cultural exaggeration of the importance of certain occupations has contributed to disappointment for those who would like to have obtained such highly esteemed jobs as physician, lawyer, or movie star, it has also contributed to the high rate of depression in those who do obtain these occupations. The excessive incidence of depression in such highly esteemed occupations is evident in their high rates of alcoholism, divorce, and suicide.

Success Depression

Success depression may result from several causes. First is the frequent attitude, instilled from childhood, that one has to be at the very top to deserve recognition or love. Second best just isn't good enough. Striving for unobtainable goals is bound to create a sense of failure when the criterion for success is always measured against someone who has done even better.

Another factor is the disappointment that can occur when happiness does not automatically materialize after the accomplishment of a long-sought goal. This is most apt to occur when other aspects of one's life have been neglected in order to attain that special objective, such as following graduation, the finalization of a big business transaction, or one's promotion at work.

Because the emotional center for mood is in one's unconscious mind, material success alone is usually inadequate to maintain continuing happiness. Since fundamental values may have been compromised, the resulting conflict of differing standards of behavior between occupational and personal life may have further promoted self-dislike and depression.

A classic example of how overemphasis on the title and

social rating of a job can result in low self-esteem is the role of housewife. It is easy to understand this since the title usually emphasizes the maintenance and cleaning of a house. Even the important responsibility of helping to raise children is not acknowledged in this label. It was the realization that these household functions were not usually considered important enough by themselves to allow full recognition of individuality that fostered the women's liberation movement. This liberation was directed at being freed from being tied down to a home, and only secondarily involved other aspects of economic, occupational, and political equality. The great emphasis made by the women's movement for obtaining regular paying jobs is evidence of our cultural priority for independence.

While the most frequent problems relating to depression in women still stem from family disappointment, it is often work-related problems that precipitate this situation in men. This not only involves disappointment in job expectations, but also results from conflict with supervisors and co-workers. Traditionally, men have been identified with their occupation and women with their husband and family. Recently, changes in the rigidity of these roles have occurred. The majority of married women now have outside jobs in addition to their family obligations. Statistics now show trends for women to have higher incidences of peptic ulcers and alcoholism. Women share with their husbands such outside job related problems as conflicts with other personnel, boredom with the job, lack of individual job recognition, and pressure to complete assignments on time. In addition, most married women still carry the major responsibility for running the household.

Occupation as Noun or Verb

An enlightening observation to reveal your attitude toward your occupation is whether you emphasize the noun (title of your job) or the verb expressing its activity. For example, if you are a physician you may more strongly identify with the title of physician, or you might more strongly emphasize the verb—practicing medicine. By saying you are a physician rather than an individual whose occupation is physician, you omit other aspects of your individuality and tend to equate total identity with this noun title. It therefore helps one to realize that no matter how important one's job is, it is only a part of one's total individuality. How different would be the implications of stating that you are the noun, housewife, versus stating that you have the responsibility to maintain a healthy physical and emotional environment to achieve the full potential for the family's well-being!

These observations should not be misconstrued to demean the importance of occupation to a balanced life. Since it demands such a major amount of our time and attention, it is an extremely important part of our individuality. It is a part and not the whole. No matter how important it may seem, it does not replace the importance of having adequate recreation and family life to balance the requirement for a healthy individuality.

Workaholics

Jeff had been practicing law for twelve years before he took a full week's vacation. No matter how upset Miriam, his wife, would become over his obsession with work, he still couldn't change. Jeff knew that it was difficult for her and the children when, night after night and weekend after weekend, he would always be working in his office. But that's the price you had to pay for success. Hard work and total dedication to the job—isn't that what his father had always told him when he was growing up? "I don't care what you become, a garbage collector or the President of the United States—I want you to be the very best," still rang in Jeff's ears. Actually, Jeff realized, his father would never have been satisfied with any occupation less important than a lawyer or a doctor. But even that wasn't enough. He had to be number one, the best, to show the world where he stood.

Jeff had to admit—but only to himself—that he didn't really enjoy his work much any more. After a while, doing the same sort of thing all the time did get boring. Especially with so little time to spend with the family, or to try a new sport or hobby, it was really quite a personal sacrifice. He couldn't under-stand why his wife was always nagging him to take some time for a vacation or recreation. Didn't she realize that their beautiful house and two expensive cars were due to all his hard work? Besides, he didn't have time for frivolous activi-ties. People only judge you by what you make of yourself, and what you have to show for it. Nothing else really counts. What if he took a two-week vacation and lost several clients? That could be the start of the collapse of his career. Word might get around that he wasn't trying to be number one any more, and that he didn't care if he lost a potential client. Well, that wouldn't happen to him. He wouldn't let it. It made him depressed even to think that he might not be considered the very best in town. And after all, he was a very successful lawyer and had to live up to that identity. The trouble with his wife was that she was only a housewife, and he might have outgrown her.

Unlike those who experience temporary overwork in the overload syndrome, workaholics continue to be chronic over-workers because of their own compulsions, not from outside pressure. In contrast to the overload syndrome, most worka-holics, like alcoholics, tend to be depressed from the start. This term should not be applied to those who must tem-porarily overwork because their job occasionally requires it. Workaholics tend to feel that their job is their entire life and their only need. Therefore, it serves to substitute for recrea-tion and diminishes the importance of family life. In other words, they depend on their job for their total individuality. This attitude will strain family relationships not only because of lack of time to spend with family activities, but because the family senses their second-class priority to the job. Another problem is that workaholics are unable to tolerate the inevi-table disappointments that occur in any job. This is due to the frequency with which compulsive workers are perfection-ists. They cannot tolerate even temporary job disappoint-ments without becoming anxious or depressed. When these setbacks at work do occur, they often have no outside inter-ests or recreation to fall back on in order to relieve tension. Their resulting moodiness and irritability will overstrain an already neglected family relationship. Since workaholics are often chronically depressed and have difficulty changing their compulsive patterns, they often require counseling. Their overwork problem is merely a symptom of a deeper under-lying problem.

Miriam couldn't understand how Jeff could be so thought-less to her and the children. Didn't she deserve some of the attention he lavished so freely on his job? After all, hadn't she slaved twenty-four hours a day, seven days a week, for their family and home? And all the help she had was a cleaning woman only once a week. With three children in school and all the responsibility to keep up the appearance of the house so everyone would know their position in the community, it wasn't easy for her. She didn't waste her time taking courses in adult ed, or flittering around on some stupid tennis court. In her own way, she worked just as hard as Jeff. And she had sacrificed just as much, or maybe even more, than Jeff. She even dropped out of that bridge club so the children wouldn't have to put up with some strange baby sitter. And even though they could have easily afforded daily cleaning help for their large house, she was willing to do most of it herself because, if you wanted a job done right, you had to do it yourself. Didn't people judge a wife by the house she kept? She wasn't going to have it said that the most successful lawyer in town had a second-rate housekeeper for a wife.

Miriam felt somehow empty and lonely. She and Jeff had not known what it meant to be lovers for a long time. With a great deal of regret, she wondered where the love that they had once shared had gone. What started out as fascination with each other as individuals had ended up as bondage to a piece of architecture for her, and a sick compulsion to a job for Jeff. In her own way, she had lost track of her own individuality just as much as her husband had. Maybe they should have made time for each other, as well as for each alone. She would ask Jeff if he would willing to get some professional help with her.

Compulsive Housewife

Another type of workaholic is the compulsive housewife. She may choose to be so preoccupied with household tasks and maternal concerns that she neglects other aspects of her individuality. This lack of adequate outside interests for recreation, education, or vocation will predispose her to depression, especially by the time the job of raising children is completed and they leave home. Not surprisingly, many compulsive worker husbands marry compulsive housewives and mothers. This term of compulsive housewife should not apply to young mothers who are temporarily overloaded by the demands of caring for small children. At least by the time the children start school, there should be some opportunity for some outside interests.

Recreation

The distinction between occupation and recreation usually depends on what you have to do to fulfill your major time-consuming responsibility. This occupation will usually occur at regular intervals for a specific period of time, and will usually result in some sort of payment, usually money but occasionally goods. In addition, there is usually a well-defined role that indicates the standards of behavior ascribed to this job. It is therefore easy to understand the special problems involved with the role of housewives. They neither work a specific amount of time nor receive any regular payment. Traditionally, they share their husbands' earnings not as a payment for services, but often as dependents receiving an allowance. With so many wives now having outside jobs, there have been understandable changes in attitudes.

Recreation is usually done at less frequent intervals and for lesser amounts of time. Its object is enjoyment rather than remuneration. The variety of its choices and its regularity of participation are often unscheduled. Its ability to offer novelty stimulation is greater than the steady routine of most jobs. The specific type of activity alone doesn't necessarily define what is recreation and what is occupation. Golf and tennis are common examples of recreation. But to those who are professionals at these sports, they are occupations. Cooking is part of the traditional work routine for the homemaker. But to her husband, who may barbecue occasionally, it is recreation.

The term "recreation" indicates "to create again." What is being re-created is a sense of total individuality—the awareness of all the aspects of one's individuality. The long hours devoted to occupational role performance tend to overemphasize that aspect of ourselves that is job related. Activities to allow fulfillment of recreational interests that relate to social, educational, and athletic needs will allow people to reestablish the total spectrum of their personalities.

Remember that it's easier to prevent the overload syndrome by anticipating your capacity and saying "no" when it is necessary than to overcommit yourself into an anxiety and/or depression state. Nevertheless, once this should occur, you could still get prompt relief by cutting out the excessive obligations. By this time, the embarrassment and guilt from having to back out can be reduced by securing your physician's recommendations to do so, thereby making it appropriately a matter of medical necessity.

On the other hand, if someone continues in an endless pattern of overwork at the expense of time for recreation and family life, then an internal workaholic compulsion may be the driving force rather than temporary external pressure. In this case, professional counseling may be required.

Recreation is necessary to help balance occupational tensions exaggerated by a society that inappropriately defines individuals only by their occupations. As in so many other depressing situations, guilt is often the major factor in both the overloader and the workaholic.

CHAPTER 6

Overcoming
the Sick Self-Image

After returning to her physician for the follow-up office visit, Mrs. B. was informed that all her lab tests and X-rays were normal and that she was in good health. Instead of being relieved, she protested emphatically that she could not accept that she was in good health since a previous physician had told her fifteen years earlier that she had five different diseases.

Miss G., a woman in her early thirties, had assumed that she had had cancer surgery for the benign disease of endometriosis because of its tendency to be found in various parts of the abdomen, even though it is never malignant.

Mr. J., a thirty-year-old man, repeatedly rushes into his physician's office complaining of palpitations, breathlessness and soreness in the chest, each time certain that he is having a fatal heart attack, and each time having a normal examination and electrocardiogram. He recalled that his mother had been concerned about his heart and had checked his pulse daily when he was a child.

Sick Self-Image

Those people who are convinced that they have a serious physical disease, even though they do not, have a condition we call "the sick self-image." This situation occurs either when they believe that they are suffering from a serious illness when, in fact, there is none, or when they have recovered from an illness but do not believe it. Most of us have experienced this at one time or another. It is very common in those who suffer from anxiety and depression and serves to aggravate these latter conditions as well as to make them worse as a result.

As discussed in a previous chapter, depression and anxiety have associated psychosomatic symptoms. The frequency in anxiety of palpitations, breathessness and chest muscle soreness may lead the person to think that he is having a heart attack; or dizziness, headache, and faintness may suggest brain disease. Functional digestive disturbances commonly mimic abdominal diseases. For the full range of symptoms, refer to the chart in Chapter 3.

Fear and Misleading Terminology

The combination of psychosomatic symptoms with pessimism from the frequent underlying depression can lead to false assumptions regarding the worst possible diseases. Convinced that he has a serious physical disease, the patient may doubt the physician's competency or honesty when informed that there is no serious disease. The fear that most people have when they consult a physician is that he might discover a serious, life-threatening illness. This fear causes distortion and misinterpretation of what the physician says, both verbally or by nonverbal mannerisms. Misunderstanding is more likely to occur when the patient is unfamiliar with the medical terms used or when the terms are confusing. It is further aggravated by the physician's need to mention every minor or unimportant finding, because of the recent greater mobility of people and the increasing frequency of medical legal suits. An example of misleading medical terminology is the electrocardiogram diagnosis of complete "right bundle branch block," which is a common normal variation and only infrequently indicates disease. One can understand the fear that may easily occur in such a patient because of the similarity in terminology to the serious disease called "complete heart block."

One patient, similarly, was greatly relieved to realize, after ten years of concern, that her diagnosis of "first degree heart block" was only a mild, relatively unimportant deviation. Since first degree murder is worse than second degree, this patient incorrectly assumed that the same must be true for heart blocks.

Disease-Focused Methods

The physician-related contributions to the sick self-image may not only result from inadequate communication between physician and patient but are often grounded in the scientific method of medical diagnosis itself. Concentrating attention on our capacity to be diseased has resulted in neglecting to train physicians in how to make a convincing diagnosis of good health in a positive manner. There can be no doubt that the remarkable scientific advances of medicine in the past century would not have been possible without its scientific, analytical, disease-focused methods. However excellent this has been for treating physical diseases, it may have distracted attention from the emotional needs of the whole person. Since the physician is trained to evaluate the patient in terms of possible diseased organs, this has led to the assumption that any symptom is due to disease until proven otherwise. In other words, we are to assume we are sick until proven healthy. If the tests are inconclusive or borderline, the patient often assumes that disease is present even though the tests more often indicate a normal variation. If the physician cannot make a definite diagnosis of the cause of the symptoms, the patient usually speculates about the most serious possibilities and is prone to develop a sick self-image. So it is important to maintain communication and contact with the physician until the disease is diagnosed or, more commonly, a psychosomatic cause can explain it.

With all the clinical, scary details of catastrophic diseases presented in the communications media, it is not surprising that anyone might assume that he could be having one of them. The medical examination is such that almost all the time is directed toward the search for possible disease, and very little toward convincing the patient that he is actually healthy. This is because we usually presume that a brief statement that the tests and examination are normal should be sufficient to inform the patient that he is healthy. But does he really believe it—especially if he has the sick self-image? For those who have recovered from previous life-threatening illnesses, their cure may be difficult to believe because of inevitably resulting anxiety or depression. In these cases it is helpful if physicians clearly emphasize the proof of cure by pointing out the clinical and laboratory evidence.

Self-Defeating Labels

The implications of a label applied to someone may make the difference between sympathetic, supportive understanding or aggravation of the underlying anxiety or depression. The most common example is the use of the socially demeaning, implicit words, *neurotic* and *hypochondriac*. The dictionary definition of hypochondriasis is "the persistent neurotic conviction that one is or is likely to become ill when illness is neither present nor likely." Since anxiety neurosis and depression both involve psychosomatic symptoms, the term *neurotic* is commonly used to mean *hypochondriac*. The main difference in the application of these terms is in how much a person overtly expresses his concern and seeks help for his symptoms. In other words, if he feels he has symptoms of possible life-threatening disease, he is usually well advised to see a physician. If the physician cannot find a physical cause for the patient's symptoms, it is often assumed by everyone concerned that he is a neurotic. If instead of suffering in silence he then continues to express his concern for the continuing symptoms, he would commonly be labeled a hypochondriac.

You may be wondering about the difference between the sick self-image and the almost identical dictionary definition of hypochondriasis. This difference lies in the implications that these two similar terms have for the involved person and the resulting contrast in attitudes that will affect his recovery. The term hypochondriac has come to mean a putdown for anyone so labeled. It invariably implies that the individual is somehow lacking in courage or strength of character and is a nuisance both to his family and to his physician. The resulting guilt that is bound to be generated reinforces the already present anxiety or depression and makes a cure that much more difficult to accomplish.

Media Sensationalism

In contrast, the concept of the sick self-image recognizes all the factors contributing to the person's illness-focused anxiety or depression. It's not the person's fault that the method and technical language of scientific medicine can predispose to this condition nor is it the person's fault that the news and entertainment media have emphasized and sensationalized catastrophic disease. It is not the person's fault that psychosomatic symptoms from the unconscious mind feel exactly the same as symptoms from serious physical disease.

In three decades of the practice of internal medicine, it has never been necessary for me to use the term "hypochondriac." Is there anyone who hasn't, at some time or other, seriously believed that he might be suffering a potentially fatal illness? All of us have been injured by society's great intolerance of functional illness. This attitude serves only to retard one's recovery and to perpetuate the condition by increasing guilt over not having a tangible physical cause.

Previous Serious Illness

A revelation finally became apparent regarding those with the most severe sick self-images who continue to display excessive concern regarding nonexistent serious physical disease in spite of previous repeated efforts to treat and educate them. In almost every such instance, their history revealed either a previous personal encounter with a potentially fatal illness that was subsequently cured, or having been suspected of having such an illness and subsequently proven not to have it. Often, this occurred as a result of some suspicious X-ray or laboratory finding that was subsequently found to be benign only after weeks or months of anxious waiting. Influential also was the effect of having experienced at close hand some relative's suffering from serious illness, often over a prolonged period of time. Perhaps if these circumstances were generally appreciated, there would be more consideration for those with the sick self-image by everyone involved—the public, friends, relatives, and that minority of physicians whose lack of understanding and patience to deal with these people has provided a mutual hardship for both physician and patient.

Doctor-Patient Communication

It would be unwise to avoid a discussion of the effect of the doctor-patient relationship on a situation so difficult to treat as the sick self-image. Admittedly, the frustration of the physician at being unable to cure his patient is exceeded only by that of his patient. Since both physician and patient have been raised in the same atmosphere of intolerance for functional illness, this prejudice will only serve to complicate the matter.

As discussed in Chapter 4, the doctor-patient relationship should be approached not as one of potential conflict, but as a partnership devoted to the same goals of good health. Each brings to this relationship different responsibilities, training, and experience. But the key to any mutually satisfying relationship is to recognize the equally important but human limitations of everyone's individuality. Then the physician need not feel inadequate if his role of physician seems compromised by failing to always cure his patients. His patient should not similarly feel guilty for not being cooperative enough to get well after a certain number of office visits. The physician will hasten improvement by restoring his patient's sense of individual worth. This will help overcome guilt and anxiety within the patient, while avoiding similar feelings of anxiety and frustration in the physician.

Similarly, by respecting the physician's and his own individuality, the patient is more likely to improve by reducing guilt about himself and anger toward his physician. This will avoid the additional stress on the sick self-image that often occurs between physician and patient in this situation. Better control of the symptoms is apt to result, and the likelihood of cure of the underlying anxiety or depression enhanced.

The most effective treatment for the sick self-image is to prevent its occurrence in the first place. While this is not always possible, it is worthwhile to try prevention since once this disease-focused anxiety or depression state develops it may be difficult to overcome. A helpful approach to its prevention, as well as treatment, encompasses an awareness of all the factors discussed in this chapter and is routinely applied during contacts with patients. These are built into the history taking and physical examination, and begin with the anticipation that anyone seeking medical attention, even during a routine health exam, has a variable amount of fear about possible discovery of some deadly or disabling disease. This fear will be capable of distorting any information transmitted to the patient by word, action, lack of communication or nonverbal mannerisms. Therefore, the language used should be simple and nontechnical, and, whenever confusion could conceivably occur, be repeated as often as seems indicated by the patient's verbal and nonverbal responses. Nothing is to be assumed; even when the patient is a physician or nurse, the same simple explanations are used. It is never assumed that the patient will take a lack of comment as an indication that the area involved is normal. While the examination is being performed, every anatomic area found to be normal is mentioned, such as, "The heart sounds are normal," or, "I feel no abnormalities on palpation of the abdomen."

Technical language is used carefully whenever appropriate, since many terms are common in the media and in discussions with friends, but it is always accompanied by at least a brief explanation in simple terms, even if not requested by the patient. Special attention is devoted to explaining situations where the benign nature of the disease could easily be misconstrued to be threatening or malignant. These include benign technical terms that sound similar to dangerous ones, as discussed earlier for various types of heart blocks.

Whenever a definite diagnosis regarding a symptom cannot be determined, or when laboratory, X-ray or ECG findings are not clearly normal, we have learned to anticipate the worst possible fears and expectations from these patients, especially after prolonged periods of anxious waiting. So other evidences for a possible benign explanation may be repeated, along with a reminder of the range of normal variations of tests and X-rays, while checking out the possibilities of serious disease. It is helpful to be able to make a positive diagnosis of anxiety or depression by their symptoms (outlined in the chart in the middle of Chapter 3) and to then explain the physiology of their psychosomatic symptoms so that the patient does not assume that he has a fatal, physical disease. It is not as reassuring to either physician or patient merely to diagnose functional psychosomatic illness by finding no objective evidence for organic physical disease, although this will at times be the only evidence available. In all fairness, it is often difficult for a physician to make a diagnosis of anxiety or depression in the first few visits. In this regard, it has been helpful, especially for the more suppressed examples of anxiety or depression, to have patients look at the anxiety-depression chart within Chapter 3 to identify key symptoms of their condition, if present.

Whenever the possibility of cancer or malignancy must be mentioned, we have been surprised how often the physician's honest use of "It's a rare possibility" is transformed by fear in the patient's mind to mean "It's a likely probability." Whenever the use of biopsy is to be considered, patients usually interpret this to indicate suspicion of malignancy even when the physician is not even remotely considering that type of illness. In these above situations, clear, easy-to-understand statements to the patient, repeated several times, including warnings that these misinterpretations are common, will often avoid the anxiety that patients might otherwise experience.

The credibility of the physician will be aided by his honesty in previous contacts with the patient. In addition, serious concentration by the physician on what his patient is saying will add much to the confidence in his competency, as well as the thoroughness with which he conducts his general examinations. This does not preclude the relief of tension afforded by a well-timed and appropriate sense of humor, but this should never be applied to the patient's symptoms or attitudes or demean the patient's individuality in any way. So the humor usually relates to situations outside of the patient's personal problems, such as the inconsistencies to be found in our society.

A paradox has been the decreased frequency with which anxious patients will call regarding psychosomatic symptoms after they have sincerely been invited to phone whenever they become concerned about their symptoms. The patients' increased sense of security afforded by this attitude decreases the panic from fear that they might not be able to contact their physician if needed. After a thorough examination and explanation, most of those with the sick self-image may call the office frequently for the first several weeks for a few minutes of reassurance. Thereafter, the calls usually diminish, often to about the same frequency as calls from other patients.

Positive Diagnosis of Good Health

Making a positive diagnosis of good health where applicable has already been discussed. It should be stressed that the sick self-image is a curable condition, even though it does require time and effort. The same approach as that for anyone with anxiety or depression will be helpful, as discussed in earlier chapters.

If nothing more than the re-establishment of self-respect and understanding for those with the sick self-image has been accomplished in this chapter, it will go a long way to help alleviate the underlying anxiety and depression state involved. It should be helpful just to realize the aggravating effects from inherently misleading terminology, indefinite diagnoses, past serious illnesses, inadequate communication, disease-focused methods, and a frightening communications media. The importance of obtaining the help of a sympathetic, concerned physician with exceptional communication skills is especially important.

CHAPTER 7

Reducing Stress from Physical Illness and Hospitalization

You're sitting in the reception room of a well-recommended physician whom you've never met, waiting for an examination regarding a recurrent abdominal pain of several months' duration.

You've just been informed that the hospital technician is ready to take you for that special X-ray examination that required your signature on the informed consent sheet, making you aware that this examination could, although rarely, cause death or injury.

You've just opened your newspaper a week before you're scheduled to have your gall bladder removed and read that hundreds of thousands of unnecessary surgical operations are performed each year.

Any illness is bound to cause at least temporary concern. Anxiety or depression often arise from just the threat of serious illness, but it is not generally appreciated how often common illnesses or surgeries cause these emotions.

Illness Stress Factors

Some of the factors that determine how much influence a particular illness may have on emotional health are the possibility that it could result in death or long-term disability; its anticipated intensity and duration; the potential for disfigurement, pain, or bodily loss; its effects on family and occupational life; and the presence or absence of anxiety or depression preceding the onset of that illness. Another important factor is the prospect for interference with such vital functions as eating, elimination, sleeping, and sex. In addition, previously held attitudes by the patient and his family regarding disease, physicians, and hospitals will help determine their reactions.

Persistent or recurrent pain not only has a direct physical effect on the production of depression but also causes a demoralizing psychological effect by suggesting that the disease may be uncontrolled or more serious than anticipated, or even that the original diagnosis may have been incorrect.

Social implications of physical illness include the loss of independence so that even such basic functions as walking, eating, talking, or eliminating might possibly require assistance from others. The possibility of being a social outcast from disfigurement, loss of control of elimination, or inability to communicate would also be a major concern.

Guilt

It is quite common for guilt feelings to develop in both the patient and his family during a serious illness or injury. It underlies such frequent questions as "Why did it have to happen to me?" or "What did I do to deserve it?" These questions reflect the frequently held but false belief that serious illness is a form of punishment for past improper behavior. In so-called primitive societies, these forces are often attributed to outside evil spirits, so guilt is less common. Many people believe that in modern Western culture these forces have become internalized through our unconscious minds so that this punishment seems to occur through psychosomatic mechanisms. Feelings of guilt not only can arise as a result of depression from physical disease, but become aggravated by concerns about inability to perform such family role functions as wage earning or homemaking. In recent years the escalating costs of health care have increased guilt and fear concerning possible financial ruin, especially in those without health insurance.

Paradoxically, it is uncommon to detect guilt feelings in those whose diseases are the result of known unhealthy habits, such as cirrhosis of the liver, which results from alcohol abuse, or pulmonary emphysema, which results from smoking. This might be related to an awareness that these habits may be beyond their conscious control, and the resulting illness occurs from factors outside their direct responsibility.

Anger

Anger may also play an important role in depression from physical illness or injury, and the family and physician are the most common targets. Like guilt, anger not only results from depression but also aggravates it. The physician is in a position similar to that of the ancient messengers whose heads were chopped off when they brought bad news to their king. It is the physician who must discover the presence of a serious disease. He can be criticized for being too honest and blunt with the bad news, or even more disliked for temporarily withholding such information. In addition to this, the pain, expense, and discomfort from the surgical or medical treatment can understandably aggravate this tendency for anger. The family is also a natural outlet for such anger since their communication is such that no pretense need be made, and deep feelings are spontaneously expressed. These are often the only socially acceptable places for the patient's anger. Since it is difficult to be the target for such anger without reacting in kind, it can be more readily handled if the physician and the family anticipate that the patient's anger is a natural result of the depression from physical disease and not take it personally.

The family and the physician may already feel somewhat guilty over unrealistic concerns of what might have been done sooner or differently. It will be helpful for them to appreciate their human limitations to predict the future. The presence of previously existing guilt-related problems within the family may serve to exaggerate these reactions. Our cultural tendency for parents to assume guilt for any problems that their children may have makes it important for the physician to reassure parents of seriously ill children that they are not to blame. It is common for children who experience prolonged or serious illness to be prone to depression later in life, so it would be helpful for the parents and the physician to allow a sick child or adult to express fears rather than suppressing them or minimizing their importance. This does not mean that the child should not be reassured and encouraged, but it does require everyone's awareness that a seriously sick child or adult is usually aware of his condition without being told.

Fear of Death

Once any person becomes aware of the seriousness of his illness by verbal or nonverbal communication, it only serves to cause more distress for someone else to initiate any further discussion about it. For most people, the greatest concern about a serious illness is the possibility of death; but in older people, it is often the fear of prolonged disability. Fear of death is often the primary source of anxiety beginning in early childhood. Its repression may contribute to anxiety and depression any time throughout life. So great is the anxiety generated by its concern that this subject is generally avoided. Even physicians may be unable to deal with this fear and, therefore, be unable to communicate adequately with their dying patients.

Terminal Illness

Recently there has been an emphasis on recognizing that the dying person has the same essential needs as any other living person. This includes the need for honest communication regarding his condition with physician and family, if desired, and the right to avoid such discussions if that is preferred. In those exceptional instances where the person indicates by word or behavior that he doesn't ever want to discuss his condition, he will usually be aware of the truth by nonverbal communication and will cooperate, accordingly, with treatment. The primary consideration should be to recognize that any person, whether healthy, sick, or dying, is still a complete human being and requires total respect for his or her individuality. This includes his likes, dislikes, feelings and behavior. Because of the limitations imposed by the illness with frequent seclusiveness and irritability, the patient often appears to undergo a change in personality. This is usually the manifestation of an understandable depression. It explains the lack of communication and spontaneity, the loss of interest in prior concerns, the lack of facial expression and slowness of movements, preoccupation with morbid concerns, and frequent insomnia and loss of appetite.

It is not uncommon for friends, relatives, and occasionally even the physician and nurses, to react to the patient's anger or seclusiveness by withdrawing from the ill person, possibly with personal feelings of rejection because of their own fears of illness and death. How often have you heard the expression, "I just hate being around hospitals or sick people"? Nevertheless, it is helpful for the family and medical personnel to make themselves available when the seriously ill person feels like talking, or just to sit quietly by if that is what is desired. It is also helpful to ask seriously ill individuals if and when they desire friends to visit, since they may not feel like putting on a pleasant front; they may be more comfortable at times just to be with close relatives. Hard as it is to believe, some people will tell a seriously ill friend about people they have known who have died from the same illness. It is also helpful for hospital visitors to request that the patient inform them when he begins to get tired, so that they will know when to leave—and to leave anyway if it is apparent that the patient is weary.

Most importantly, keep in mind that there is no state-of-being known as dying. This describes a stage of disease, not of life. So either you are living or you are dead. And until you are dead, you are totally alive even though your illness may be at a terminal stage. Obviously, no one wants to be treated as if he or she were already dead so the crux of the matter is to treat even the most seriously ill people with the same consideration for their total individuality that one would for anyone else. That may even include using an appropriate sense of humor when the ill person desires it. It certainly requires the consideration not to have one's needs dictated by others. It is heartening that death is no longer a forbidden, repressed subject. Accepting this stage as one of living may be an important factor in decreasing the hardship of such a difficult situation.

Hospital Depersonalization

Hospital experiences will often serve to aggravate the loss of individuality and depression already brought on by a serious disease. The necessary regimentation of busy institutions will often erode the basic rudiments of self-identity. Even the term *patient* usually suggests a subservient status; someone to be told what to do by a higher authority. Depersonalization (loss of personal identity) is exemplified by the necessity to be assigned a hospital number and the exchange of individualized clothing for a uniform hospital gown. Such private matters as eating, sleeping, and elimination become routinely recorded information on the hospital nursing chart. Even the most simple preferences and habits are subject to disapproval by nurses and physicians, including what and when to eat; the frequent restriction of alcoholic drinks, smoking, coffee or tea; where and when one may come and go; the amounts and kinds of exercise; and the simple responsibility of taking one's own medication if one is able. Regimentation even limits the nurses, who are not even allowed to use their medical knowledge to give a patient aspirin without a physician's order—yet any child can buy it in a drug store.

Depersonalization further results from not being prepared for the many wonders of the diagnostic world, which can be overwhelming. The whole array of X-ray, laboratory, nuclear and electrical tests have offered great benefits in proper diagnosis and treatment. Loss of personal identity could be minimized by having patients properly prepared to anticipate experiences such as the discomfort of prolonged immobilization on hard diagnostic tables or the use of strong laxatives and enemas. No hospital should ever tolerate indifference, rudeness, or lack of consideration by any employee, professional or otherwise. The emotional strains of a prolonged hospitalization, the discomfort from disease or surgery, and the depersonalization resulting from hospital regimentation may result in a condition commonly known to physicians and nurses as "hospitalitis." This is characterized by irritability, anger, and depression in patients who have been exposed to these forces longer than they can tolerate. Usually, it occurs only after the patient has sufficiently recovered from his acute pain and disability so that he can either be sent home or be transferred to a room with more privacy and freedom of movement.

The unfortunately frequent error of constructing intensive care and coronary care units without windows deprives patients of the biorhythmic awareness of day and night and—along with the lack of privacy, continuous lighting and hustle and bustle—may result in this anxiety-depression coming on in a few days, often in association with confusion in older patients.

The medical necessity for hospitals, diagnostic tests, and special-care units cannot be challenged. The steady dedication with which most nurses perform their responsibilities, in spite of difficult demands from patients, physicians, and supervisors, has earned them a highly respected reputation. Their intuitive responses to the patients' individuality and emotional and physical needs are an important factor in the patient's recovery from serious illness. Since most hospital personnel and physicians do the best that they are able, the problems involved in hospital regimentation are not the fault of anyone, but are inherent in the modern technical scientific system of medical diagnosis and treatment that has resulted in the highest recovery rate from serious illness ever achieved.

Nevertheless, much can be done to respond to the emotional needs of those exposed to the stress of serious physical disease or surgery. First of all, everyone—patient, family, and professionals—should anticipate the emotional impact and be prepared to prevent or reduce any anger, guilt, and depression that may occur as a result. Allowing for the appropriateness and prompt expression of these emotions will provide relief and prevent further misunderstanding between patient, family, and physicians. Hospital personnel and physicians are becoming more sensitive to patients' emotional needs and more emphasis is being devoted to considering the patient as a whole person.

To reduce hospital regimentation, there have been recent attempts in some hospitals towards more personalized care by assigning nurses and aides complete care for a smaller number of patients. Further individualization of patients could be achieved without loss of safety or efficiency by such simple choices as a variety of hospital gowns and pajamas and, possibly, the patient's taking on more responsibility for his own care while in the hospital, if he is capable of doing so. This would certainly allow more time for overworked nurses to perform other tasks, while at the same time reducing possibilities of a patient getting someone else's medication. Many hospitals now offer a choice of menus and even allow a glass of wine when it is not medically restricted.

Erosion of Doctor-Patient Relationship

Anxiety about disease has been increased in recent years by prejudice toward the medical profession. This harm is not limited just to individual physicians, but threatens the health of everyone concerned by undermining the bond of faith within the individual doctor-patient relationship. This bond, like any other, is based on mutual respect for each other's individuality, the awareness of realistic expectations and human limitations, and the uncompromised, sincere efforts of everyone concerned. The potential life-and-death decisions to be made, along with the emotionally charged intimate information shared, make this relationship second to none in terms of sensitivity and importance.

The key to solving this dilemma lies in the meaning of the phrase, *doctor-patient relationship.* Notice that this isn't called the *medical profession-patient relationship.* When you consult your physician, you are not dealing with a group. A physician, like anyone else, is first, last, and foremost an individual. His group affiliation with other physicians allows for his training, certification, and consultations; but he ultimately must exercise his skills as an individual working with another individual—the patient.

Any decisions, actions, and, rarely, personal errors in judgment that may occur will be the physician's personal responsibility as an individual. No consultant, government official, guidebook, or medical association will be able to usurp the physician's personal responsibility to his patient nor make the kinds of sacrifices for his time and emotional involvement that are usually taken for granted.

Paradoxically, the prejudice against the medical profession as a group is not usually applied to one's own individual physician, He's usually taken to be an exception, the "nice guy" in a group of opportunists. The reality of the situation is that there is no uniform medical profession.

Recently, there has been a healthy trend for patients to share with their physicians a greater responsibility for making decisions regarding testing and alternatives in treatments. Obviously, the physician will so indicate when there are no reasonable alternatives. It is rare to experience any casualties as a result of allowing fuller awareness and participation in decision-making by patients. After all, it is their lives that are being subjected to evaluation and treatment. This increased sense of responsibility afforded to patients only stimulates their greater cooperation and dedication to preventing further disease by healthier ways of living.

Being prepared to handle stress from illness, hospitalization, or disability requires increased awareness of all factors by everyone concerned: patient, family, and professionals. These stressful influences include uncertainties regarding survival, disability, pain and suffering, bodily loss, and possibly impairment as spouse, wage earner, or family member. It is imperative for everyone dealing with the ill person to use clear, supportive communication that will not be easily misunderstood—a frequent problem because of associated anxiety and/or depression. Anticipating the frequency of anger and guilt from the patient or family during serious illness will help the physician, hospital personnel or other family members to deal with it without becoming angry, guilty, or withdrawn themselves. Finally, the potential loss of individuality from hospitalization, diagnostic procedures, or label of terminal illness can be minimized by appropriately concerned consideration by professionals and aides, and by treating the seriously and terminally ill as important, living individuals.

CHAPTER 8

How to Prevent Social Drinking from Becoming Problem Drinking

Staring at the floor of his physician's office, Sam couldn't deny it: he liked the feeling that followed a few drinks. Not that he ever got drunk, but why shouldn't he loosen up and relieve his work tension for a few hours at night? Everybody did it.

He couldn't understand why his wife insisted that he discuss his drinking habits with his family physician when he had his checkup. It wasn't his problem; it was hers. When his doctor asked if his wife ever said that he seemed like a different person after a few drinks, Sam replied that this was her major concern. But he couldn't even remember having behaved belligerently or crudely after a few drinks, as she described, nor being unable to participate in a reasonable conversation. What did she take him for anyway, one of those rare split personalities?

He had to admit that it was possible that the alcohol clouded his awareness of his own behavior, especially since he often couldn't remember what had occurred the night before. Sam recognized that his wife was not the type to call wolf if there wasn't any problem. And he was aware of a growing dependency on his drinking and readily admitted that he was gradually increasing the amounts of alcohol used over the years, along with a tendency to be more depressed.

After a few drinks at parties, he had occasionally embarrassed his wife by making obvious passes at some of the other wives or started pointless arguments using crude language. But he didn't consider himself the sterotyped alco-holic—the skid row bum who drinks from morning till night. And he could go without a drink for days, or even a few weeks. But he certainly had a problem related to drinking—his wife was threatening to leave him. As his physician observed, when you have a drinking problem not just the amounts taken, but the problems resulting that are the tip-off. Sam would have to do some serious soul-searching and get his priorities in order. He knew that it wasn't an easy task to quit drinking when one became dependent on its sedation, but he didn't want to lose his wife either.

Drinking habits can be one of the most difficult to change. After someone has already developed an obvious alcohol dependency, there is often little that that person can do alone to help himself. By this time the only effective solution may be to seek help from Alcoholics Anonymous or treatment centers. The individual must do this himself. No one can force him.

Depression and Alcohol

The relationship of alcohol dependency to depression is very close. In fact, it is rare to encounter alcoholism without associated depression. It makes no dffference which came first. Alcohol excess is a chemical cause of depression and it can also lead to alcoholism in those who are so predisposed. Thus alcoholism and depression may progress together. The label *alcoholic* is misleading, since many people think that this represents one who is continuously intoxicated. Actually, it represents anyone who has any alcohol-related problem, no matter how frequent or how much alcohol is used. The term *alcohol dependency* represents a person's inability to per-manently stop drinking when it becomes apparent to him or to others that he is having problems related to the use of alcohol.

Social Drinking—Three Types

It should not be surprising that the vast majority of the ten million Americans with major alcohol problems began not as hard drinkers but as social drinkers. The crux of the problem is the total lack of any definition for social drinking, and the term itself implies not only cultural acceptance but also its promotion for social group activities. Therefore, what is social drinking? What are the actual amounts involved? And what are the guidelines? First of all, there are neither definitions, guidelines, nor definite limits. Little attention has been paid to social drinking as a potential problem. Most of the attention has been directed to the obviously advanced and difficult-to-treat disease called alcoholism. This focus has only promoted the false sense of security afforded by the cover label of "social drinker." Being aware of what type of social drinker you may be may allow for possible prevention of problem drinking, since it will be more difficult to help yourself after your brain has been chronically affected by overuse of alcohol.

Social Ritual and Food Accompaniment

We have categorized social drinking as including three main types. The first is drinking as a social function—performing a common ritual with others. The second is for alcohol's use as a food accompaniment, usually in the form of beer or wine with the meal. And the third type is drinking for its pharmacological sedative and transient mood-elevating effects on one's brain. Of course, several of the above reasons can be operating at any one time. The social ritual of a before-dinner or party drink can be accomplished by taking only one drink of alcohol, and the food-complement usage of alcohol can be obtained with only one glass of beer or wine.

Pharmacological Social Drinking

The springboard to alcohol dependency may rest on using alcohol for the third reason listed above—its pharmacologic effect—without realizing it. This self-deception can occur because of the common cover-up label of "social drinking." This label further suggests that if you don't participate you're antisocial. An analogy of drinking for its drug effect can be compared to the way tranquilizers or sedative drugs are used medically. Here, the dosage (amount), duration of treatment, frequency of intake, and selection of which drugs are prescribed are supervised by an objective physician and obtained through the services of a second double-checking professional, the pharmacist. This controlled situation is clearly understood to be a treatment for a medical reason, with all the usual precautions taken to prevent potentially dangerous side effects.

In the case of social drinking taken for its relaxing or sedative effects, there are no outside professionals to supervise safe dosage or frequency, nor be alert to unhealthy side effects. This is left entirely to the individual consuming the alcohol. He is not only unaware that he is treating himself for a medical condition—usually anxiety and often depression—but the more he drinks the worse will become his anxiety and depression the next day, even though he feels initially relieved for a few hours. Self-controlling judgment will usually be lost after a few drinks, while the realization that he is actually using a drug would never occur to him.

The cocktail party is an established American tradition. And how can you have a good time at a party without loosening up? You wouldn't want to appear different from the others at a party—would you? It's easy to see the cultural group pressures inherent in these clichés.

Although many pharmacologic social drinkers manage to avoid gross intoxication, many become conditioned to repeatedly seeking transient relief from tension, whether alone or at parties, by using alcohol for its sedative effect. What they do not realize is its more prolonged depressing effect the next day after the transient sense of well-being or tranquilization wears off. When the strain of everyday tensions builds up, the likelihood of using larger amounts of alcohol to temporarily alleviate larger amounts of anxiety or depression is then a conditioned response. Since alcohol is an addicting drug, one gradually becomes immune (tolerant) to its sedating effect at lower amounts (doses) and one has to consume larger and larger amounts to achieve the original degree of sedation. This situation produces the vicious cycle of increasing amounts of alcohol increasing the severity of anxiety and depression, which then causes further increase in the amount of alcohol used for temporary sedation.

If alcohol is not depended upon for sedative purposes in the first place, it is not likely to be used in larger amounts when greater stress occurs. How to avoid this vicious cycle is simply not to drink alcohol for its sedative effects. And this can be accomplished by limiting oneself to no more than one drink a day. This would still allow for the social ritual as well as the food-accompaniment functions of alcohol. If one complains that he cannot become relaxed with only one drink, he is confirming the fact that he is using alcohol for its sedative, pharmacologic effect. For those with alcoholism already present, even one drink is too much.

If, for any reason, one prefers not to drink at all, it would seem foolish to force oneself to do so, even though this seems

difficult in a group-dependent culture that seemingly dis-
approves of total abstinence. After all, "teetotaler" was not
originally intended to be a complimentary label, but the
trends are toward improvement in this situation.

As a simple guide, problem drinking occurs when one
drinks more than he can afford—medically, socially, mari-
tally, financially, occupationally, or emotionally. If any of
these functions are being compromised as a result of alcohol
usage, you can assume you've got a problem. All of the other
mind-altering drugs are appropriately labeled "dangerous" or
"illegal," but any amount of alcohol can be obtained and
used without regard to health or law—unless one gets caught
while driving drunk.

A Safe Limit

If alcohol were discovered today, the Federal Drug Ad-
ministration would not allow it to be sold or would require a
physician's prescription, but the reality of the situation is
that alcohol is here to stay. Perhaps if there were more
understanding of the various types of social thinking, some
reduction in this common type of drug dependency might be
accomplished. Limiting oneself to only one ordinary drink a
day may seem simplistically unsophisticated, but it may be
the surest protection available short of total abstinence.

It is especially important to avoid alcohol or to adopt a
limit of only one drink for those with anxiety or depression
because these are the ones most predisposed to its depressing effects, even in small amounts. They are also the ones
most likely to seek out the temporary sedation afforded by its
pharmacologic effects.

What about those who already have an obvious drinking
problem, recognized either by themselves or by their families? Experience confirms the conviction of Alcoholics
Anonymous, that total abstinence is the only effective means
for those with alcohol problems, for reasons that will be
described.

Disease of Alcoholism

Since it is difficult to define alcoholism in terms of just the
amounts used, you will know that you have a drinking
problem when it has contributed to any health problems,
marital stress, impaired work performance, caused social

embarrassment to you or your family, caused financial strain, or contributed to your anxiety or depression. Examples of physical diseases resulting from alcohol are numerous, as outlined in the case history below. Almost every system of the body can be involved. Even a memory blackout of the evening before, or a hangover the next morning, is an indication of a disease process whose repetition could result in chronic illness.

Ann was highly insulted that her physician would even consider the possibility that she could have a drinking problem. After all, how could she have been so successful as chairperson of all those volunteer committees if that were so? Those abnormal liver tests found during her routine checkup could be due to a virus—even her physician admitted that. But to question her in detail about her drinking habits—as if she might be some sort of common alcoholic!

Sure, she had a cocktail or two at the committee luncheons—like anyone else. And what was she to do when her husband came home from a trying day at the office and wanted to relax with a few before-dinner drinks—just stare at him while he drank alone? She never had gotten drunk in her whole life, and she always handled her liquor well. Even at a party, she could put away three to five drinks and no one would be the wiser.

She finally was made to acknowledge that whether or not the liver became damaged by alcohol was not determined by any mental or behavioral changes. Her physician told her that medical science doesn't know why some people get cirrhosis of the liver from drinking less than others who escape this disease and drink more; nor why others develop peptic ulcers, pancreatitis, brain atrophy (early senility), neuritis, convulsions, or delirium tremens (a toxic hallucinating psychosis). The major point, emphasized her physician, is that anything more than a single daily drink of anything is a little like playing Russian roulette. You never know when or where you'll be injured, and, if you play the game long enough, the chances of getting hurt become higher.

Ann finally realized that her physician was not moralizing,but was offering sound medical advice no different than if she had emphysema and he were suggesting that she quit smoking. She was greatly relieved to learn that early liver damage from alcohol almost always disappears after total, complete cessation of drinking.

It doesn't make any difference if your drinking problem

occurs daily or only once a month. If it hurts you or your family, you have a problem. If you have a drinking problem, even one drink will be too much, since sooner or later it will lead to more.

Dual Personality

Why can't you stop drinking by yourself? Supposedly, all it takes is making up your mind. The paradox is that you really don't have just one mind—you have two. This may be hard to believe, but is obvious to anyone who has lived with someone with an alcohol problem. The kind, soft-spoken, reliable Dr. Jekyll often turns into a brutal, vulgar Mr. Hyde after imbibing only relatively small amounts of alcohol. It was Robert Louis Stevenson's awareness of the duality of human behavior that led him to write his classic story. While there is no historical evidence that Stevenson was specifically thinking of alcohol, the coincidence of the liquid potion causing the dramatic personality change is remarkable.

This dual personality can arise from any emotional problems, especially depression, and results from conflicting attitudes between the socially concerned, conscious mind and a sick unconscious mind, with resulting different patterns of behavior depending on which mind is dominant at the time. In the case of alcohol dependency, the socially proper conscious mind is suppressed by the alcohol. If the depressed unconscious mind contains suppressed anger, as is often the case in alcoholism, hostile behavior results. Paradoxically, many of those who have alcohol problems rarely show anger when sober and are often known as the "nicest" people. The alcoholic is not lying the next morning when his sober conscious mind swears that he will never drink again. He feels guilty and really means what he is promising. But his unconscious mind is alcohol dependent and will take over and seek out alcohol whenever his conscious resistance is weakened by fatigue, frustration, or even one drink of alcohol.

The disease of alcoholism is a variety of depression most likely associated with a hereditary, biochemical predisposition to this illness. Since half of those who suffer from this disease have parents or siblings who are similarly affected, it seems unlikely that they would have wanted, even unconsciously, to imitate this very unpleasant behavior.

Why A. A. Helps

The most successful approach to overcoming problem drinking has been through joining Alcoholics Anonymous. There are several reasons for this. First of all, A.A.'s program relieves guilt by teaching that alcoholism is a disease rather than a sin or a crime. How can you be judged morally for a disease over which you have no conscious control? It is guilt that deepens the depression that causes further conditioned drinking. It is guilt that also prevents one from facing the truth of such a painful realization. Alcoholics Anonymous functions to reeducate one's unconscious mind to cure itself of a drug-associated depression, with regular group therapy meetings. It promotes facing reality by having the member admit that he is an alcoholic. It recognizes that everyone is responsible for his behavior. It is his or her decision to come to meetings and to stop drinking. No one is forcing the issue.

Unlike most organizations, Alcoholics Anonymous exists entirely to help its individual members and is not an organization to promote its own image. It helps its members overcome depression, first by abstaining from the drug effects of alcohol, and at the same time by increasing their sense of self-worth. This elevation of low self-image is accomplished by reducing guilt, encouraging individual responsibility, sharing similar feelings and experiences with others, and providing the opportunity to help others with a similar problem. Completely eliminating the drug effect of alcohol on the brain allows the return of the ability of this organ to carry out healthy, commonsense decisions. Whether or not one seeks out professional counseling in addition, it is no substitute for Alcoholics Anonymous since most psychologists and psychiatrists recognize that this organization has developed the most successful approach to this problem. This doesn't mean that counselors or other organizations cannot be of additional help.

Alcohol is the most commonly abused mind-altering drug in our society, but this does not mean that unhealthy use of any other mind-altering drugs is any less dangerous. This includes the use of any such drugs as LSD, marijuana, cocaine, uppers and downers. Even prescribed tranquilizers, sedatives, and sleeping pills can be harmful if used in greater amounts than prescribed, or occasionally, in some people, even when taken as directed. The frequent or daily use of marijuana may result in brain dysfunction similar to that occurring with the regular, intoxicating use of alcohol.

There can be little doubt of the major contribution that intoxicating drugs like alcohol have made to the psychometabolic blues. This includes not only depression, anxiety, and fatigue, but also a wide variety of personal and social problems such as criminal acts, family disruption and divorce, loss of employment, and the widest variety of physical diseases known to be caused by a single agent.

Therefore, the only way to use alcohol safely is to remain fully aware that it is a potent drug, that its potentially harmful effects upon the brain and body can usually be prevented by limiting use of it to only a single drink a day, and that social drinking to relax or unwind is really using alcohol as an actual drug without the supervision of a physician or pharmacist. Once you're caught in the disease of alcoholism, the most successful treatment involves the help of Alcoholics Anonymous, in addition to whatever professional help you may obtain.

As for the relatives of those with alcohol problems, Al Anon is an A.A.-related organization with meetings to help people close to alcoholics deal with the problem. Books and organizations devoted to the problems of adult children of alcoholics have received a lot of attention recently. There are many publications now about co-dependency, a term used to describe the addiction-permitting role of those who live with alcohol and drug-addicted persons. The enormous incidence of alcohol and drug addiction in recent decades is evidenced by the voluminous literature on recovery from drug and alcohol abuse.

CHAPTER 9

Overcoming the Fat Self-Image

She just stood there on the office scales, eyes shut tightly, hands clenched into fists and body held rigidly, as if waiting to be executed by a firing squad. One would have expected the scales to register at least fifty pounds overweight by her reaction, but, as pointed out to her later, her weight fell within the normal range and was only several pounds over the median. But Carolyn could not be reassured. "Just look at the shape of my abdomen," she exclaimed, "and my hips—what about them?" Actually, most everyone would have agreed that she was an attractive woman with a shape that most would envy. But when these observations had been offered during previous checkups, they resulted only in accusations of our being dishonest and patronizing.

Actually, Carolyn seemed to have everything that anyone could desire except self-confidence. Her husband continued to be just as affectionate as he was when they had gotten married fifteen years earlier, and other men usually looked twice at her when they met her. She was really an attractive woman; so why did she continue to believe that she was so fat and ugly? And why couldn't she accept what seemed so obvious to everyone else?

Double Standard Regarding Overweight

Why do we encounter in women such frequent overreaction to weight? Don't men have the same problem? Certainly, but our society has produced such a double standard about overweight that even the women's liberation movement hasn't challenged it. Of course, it is unhealthy for men to be overweight, but in women it is considered a deplorable abhorrence as well. These women are not only outcasts from

99

fashion styles but, even more importantly, they often consider themselves very unattractive and find it harder to get a good job or a husband. Many overweight women suffer from guilt and depression as a result of this attitude, which itself often causes more overeating and depression.

This modern-day social bias has produced an epidemic of depressing "fat self-image" among the American female population, including not only overweight women, but many normal or even underweight women. Some of them have been heavy at one time and retain a false conviction that they are still heavy. Others who are of normal weight compare themselves to the skinny models who display their emaciated shapes in magazine ads. The vast majority of all women seen for any reason in medical practice carry some degree of this self-imposed put-down regarding weight.

There's not much anyone can do to change the attitudes of those with normal weight who have a fat self-image. Since most of them are not severely affected, they will not usually require psychotherapy. A minority with severe emotional problems, like those with starvation-prone anorexia nervosa,* will require treatment. But the majority will get by with patience from their families and, hopefully, there may be some changes in our cultural attitudes in the future.

Should the millions of overweight people be educated to accept their condition? First of all, it won't work; the bias against overweight is just too strong. The most compelling reason for maintaining a normal weight is the overwhelming evidence that it promotes better health. Diabetes, high blood pressure, heart disease and even cancer are more common in obesity. So for both mental and physical reasons, it is healthful to maintain a normal weight. Nevertheless, the harm to emotional health by guilt and depression resulting from anti-weight prejudice is of epidemic proportions.

---

*It is beyond the scope and experience of this book to discuss in detail the disease known as *anorexia nervosa*. This psychiatric illness is usually characterized by severe weight loss, averaging 40 percent of body weight, not due to physical organic causes; loss of menstrual periods; onset most often in teenage girls or young women; and an exaggerated fat self-image. It requires treatment by experienced psychiatrists or psychologists. It has been increasing in incidence, perhaps as a result of our cultural bias for slimness in women. *Bulemia* is a related disorder in which women who are desperate to lose weight induce vomiting or diarrhea in order to accomplish it.

Since so many different schemes for losing weight have been tried, it is obvious that there has been no simple, totally satisfactory solution. Those who have a long history of significant overweight usually regain their weight sooner or later, no matter how they lose it, and the long-term success rate has been compared to that of many incurable diseases.

An Effective Solution

But a method that has been very successful in helping people achieve and maintain a normal weight has been verified personally in hundreds of cases over a ten-year period. First of all, to convince the person to follow such a program, he or she is made to realize that one should not feel guilty about being overweight. Guilt, itself, will often prevent the person from doing something about it. Although many chronically overweight people try hard to lose and maintain weight reduction, most end up eventually with failure. There is no doubt that they consciously want to lose weight, perhaps more than anything else in the world.

The crux of the problem is this: they should not feel guilty, because they have no direct conscious control over the situation. The fundamental disturbances underlying chronic obesity lie in the unconscious mind and include frequent depression as well as poorly understood biochemical and genetic factors that commonly cause overweight people to gain more easily than others.

Like such other variable physiologic measurements as blood pressure, temperature and pulse, the controlling center for appetite and weight is in the deep brain stem called the hypothalamus. Here occur switchboard-like connections between the conscious cerebral cortex and the autonomic nervous system to coordinate food intake and its metabolism. The hypothalamus is also intimately connected with the master endocrine gland, the pituitary, which controls the function of other glands, including the thyroid and adrenal, which influence the rate at which body fat is broken down. Even though we do not currently know how to measure the individual differences in rate of fat production, it is apparent from controlled calorie intake studies that overweight individuals gain more fatty weight from the same intake of calories than do persons of normal weight—confirming what overweight people have been claiming for years, and there is the possibiliy also that the tendency for overweight runs in families.

Does that mean that nothing can be done about it? Certainly not. A highly successful program of supervised diet instruction and regular weight checks in an atmosphere free of guilt is readily available. These are offered by organizations such as Weight Watchers and involve weekly meetings, private weigh-ins, and learning about nutrition, along with using a sensible, balanced diet. After the weight becomes normal, attending meetings only once a month usually helps prevent the recurrence of overweight.

Freaky, bizarre diets may allow weight loss but are usually not successful in maintaining normal weight because one eventually tires of them. The use of drugs to lose weight is of little help because of possible side effects, eventual loss of effectiveness, and the need to depend on these drugs indefinitely.

Jeanette was thoroughly disgusted. While her husband ate exactly the same amount of food she did, he remained slim and she stayed thirty pounds overweight. She knew no one believed that she hardly ever snacked—not her friends, not her husband, not even her physician. As long as she could remember, people had quoted that the only way to become fat was to overeat. Yet the only times that she had been able to lose were when she went on a semistarvation diet, or one where you could eat no carbohydrate at all. Then she gained it all back as soon as she couldn't stand it any more. She thought she had tried everything—pills, shots, and every new fad diet that appeared in magazines and books.

And she wasn't going to make a fool out of herself by going to those group weekly meetings and be seen in public with all those overweight people. Besides, she didn't have time to go to meetings; she was too busy. Just the thought of having to appear at a weekly meeting for fat people—ugh!

Six months after her doctor finally persuaded her to go to those weight reduction meetings and follow a diet that wasn't freaky, she had to admit that maintaining her now normal weight was easy, as long as she had the monthly maintenance contact and weigh-in at the meeting place. So what if it was a little like being dependent on A.A.? It worked.

It is a paradox that those who are most severely overweight are often the ones who are most resistant to an effective group program such as Weight Watchers. Their reasons cannot usually be verbalized. Often this resistance relates to the person's extreme guilt about excessive weight, resulting in inability to consciously face the problem—similar to an alcoholic's difficulty in admitting his problem. Explaining why they should not feel guilty has allowed many with this problem to accept help from these groups.

Since it is up to the individual to decide what to do about excess weight, it only causes resentment for a family member to pressure him or her. Obesity, like alcoholism, may not only result from mental stress, but also contribute to it.

Exercise Benefits

Regular exercise is an important aid to weight control. It does burn extra calories, even though it is often said that the amount of calories burnt up is relatively small. But it seems that exercise trains the body to metabolize food more efficiently, perhaps by converting less carbohydrate to fat. Major benefits of regular exercise are its improvement in energy and its antianxiety and antidepression effects. Other benefits are increased muscle tone and decreased sagging of the skin previously stretched by fat. What kind of exercise is best? It really doesn't matter as long as one does it regularly, preferably daily, or at least every other day. It should include some whole body motion involving the legs, such as walking or swimming. Calisthenics can also be helpful. It is important not to engage in too vigorous activity before one's condition allows it to be done safely. Except for young people in good health, jogging should be reserved for those who have been cleared by their physician, possible after an exercise electro-cardiogram.

For the individual who seems too busy to find the time to exercise, there is a solution. We have a cultural habit that could be used. Eating three meals a day made sense when our ancestors worked hard from sunrise to sunset. Now, the vast majority of us lead sedentary lives. Since the lunch hour is usually available, one could take a brisk walk during this time, eating a piece of fruit or cheese as the lunch. One could have a balanced breakfast and supper and get the benefit of a reduced lunch, with the added exercise.

Associated Diseases

Physical diseases such as hypothyroidism are quite rare as causes of overweight, but a medical exam is still worthwhile to rule out other diseases that may be associated with overweight, such as high blood pressure, diabetes, or heart disease. Overweight can also be due to taking excess calories in the form of alcohol. Stopping or reducing the alcohol may be all that is necessary, but this may be difficult because of alcohol dependency.

Prejudice Against the Overweight

From the viewpoint of health, the goal of normal weight cannot be challenged. At the same time, social prejudice against overweight has inflicted immeasurable emotional harm to many people, especially women, whether they are really overweight or not. Our arbitrary standard that equates beauty with slimness is not to be found in any other culture nor at any other time in history. All one needs to do to verify this is to go to an art museum. The paintings of the Renaissance, the ancient Greek and Roman statues, and Oriental art forms depict female beauty with proportions that would be considered overweight in our present society.

Like most other prejudices, that against overweight has no justification. Health is entirely a private, personal matter. As far as others are concerned, one's health potential is no one else's business, unless they are close relatives. Any disregard of the right to be any weight one happens to be is an affront to one's individuality.

It is important, therefore, for anyone concerned about overweight to realize the inappropriateness of this social bias. It is especially important for women to become aware of the unfair double standard of weight intolerance that they might have to contend with. Finally, it is necessary to recognize the disease of chronic overweight for what it is—a disease that has usually responded best to the types of supportive programs offered by Weight Watchers and Overeaters Anonymous.

CHAPTER 10

Controlling Excessive Guilt from Family Loss, Conflict, and Disappointment

Phyllis had always felt that her son, Frank, was not just an ordinary boy. Even as a young child, he seemed capable of understanding ideas and feelings that escaped even some adults. Their relationship to each other was even closer than she had with her husband. In fact, she had realized shortly after she had married that she had chosen a man who would never really understand her needs, feelings, and sensitive nature. But after her son was born, it didn't really make any difference. Frank would come to her whenever he was upset, like the day he came home from his first day in kindergarten. He just couldn't stop hugging her. Phyllis needed someone to care and depend on her and to show love and affection. She had already accepted her husband as a "cold fish," but as long as she had her little boy, she could get along without her husband's affection. Frank would be the "real man" in her life.

Family Guilt and Depression

A famous anthropologist once defined the American family as an institution for the promotion of emotional illness. Like most exaggerations, this one had an element of truth, because the most frequent event to precede the onset of depression is either the loss of or a major disappointment with a member of the immediate family. This includes loss by

105

death or divorce as well as disappointment, particularly in expectations regarding children. To a lesser degree, this can even occur when children merely grow up and leave home as a natural course of events. Loss through divorce is now frequent.

The most important factor influencing whether or not loss or disappointment will result in depression will be the amount of guilt that develops. This in turn will depend on the quality of the relationship before the event, the immediate circumstances surrounding that event, and whether there was some depression already existing.

Normally one experiences some degree of guilt under any circumstance of loss or disappointment, but it is the intensity and duration of guilt that can make the difference. Even an eighty-year-old parent continued to feel so guilty and depressed over her fifty-year-old daughter's alcoholism that she required psychotherapy. She wondered what she did or did not do during the raising of her child to cause this addiction. The parent-child relationship does not disappear even with old age.

Mourning and Depression

When a family member is lost through death, the immediate reaction is often guilt over what could have been done to foresee and prevent it. This guilt occurs whether or not there is any personal responsibility involved. Differentiating the depression that occurs as a part of normal mourning from that which is clinically abnormal cannot usually be determined immediately after the death of a family member. The intensity of the sadness and the occurrence of psychosomatic symptoms such as loss of appetite and insomnia are identical. At times, feelings of guilt may seem more intense in those who will go on to develop the more prolonged abnormal depression. In every sense, mourning is a period of intense depression, but its duration is limited to an appropriate period for the particular circumstance. Usually, this is up to several months for the major symptoms, with lesser degrees of depression lasting for one to two years. If the duration of the intense period of depression persists more than a few months, with continuing severe psychosomatic symptoms, then one might be experiencing a true clinical depression and should seek benefit from professional help; otherwise, the depression might persist for years. Even for normal mourning, it is often helpful to see one's personal physician for whatever support could be offered.

The quality of the relationship before death can be a great influence. Paradoxically, we have observed that the death of a spouse in a happy marriage may be less likely to cause prolonged depression than in an unhappy marriage. Also, a surviving son or daughter is less likely to experience prolonged depression if there had been a comfortable relationship with the parent. These observations might be explained by the amount of guilt generated by regrets over unresolved conflicts. Unselfish love may be the capacity to let go of a loved one if it should be necessary.

The immediate circumstances surrounding the death of a family member will also influence the amount of guilt generated. It may seem obvious that a suicide involving marital conflict may generate more guilt than death from natural causes. What may not be obvious is that the suicide and the marital stress may have had the same underlying cause—depression in the one who committed suicide. Often this is related primarily to factors outside of the marriage, and the surviving spouse assumes a burden of guilt that is not deserved. Even when a spouse dies of natural causes, the survivor often feels that he or she should have sought medical help sooner, or somehow have foreseen the problem.

Another important circumstance is whether the survivor has had an opportunity to prepare for the death of the loved one. Sudden, unexpected death, without a preceding period of illness, may not allow the psychological preparation afforded by a chronic illness. The disbelief and denial that often follows prevents the usual expression of grief and may predispose one to the development of a delayed onset of depression.

Prolonged Nursing

We have also observed prolonged depression in those who take on the unselfish responsibility of nursing a chronically ill relative. It was unexpected to observe the amount of depression in a surviving wife who had faithfully nursed her eighty-year-old husband for twenty years before he died. Another example was the depression in a seventy-year-old woman who had nursed her totally paralyzed daughter in a respirator at home for thirty years before the daughter died. If any had reason not to feel guilty, it was these people, yet they felt that they were somehow responsible for the deaths of their loved ones. This inappropriate assumption of guilt under these circumstances occurs as a result of total commitment and dedication. The day-and-night preoccupation allows no time for relief from the demanding and often depressing situation. The overload of responsibility further predisposes to the depression of the survivor, even before the death occurs. Afterward, the depression becomes overt, since its expression beforehand would have been upsetting to the dying relative. While no one would want to discourage people from such admirable devotion, some recreation and relief should be obtained. These individuals should also be prepared to anticipate and cope with this extra, undeserved burden of guilt.

The mood of the survivor before the death of the relative is another important factor in the development of prolonged depression. If the survivor had been significantly depressed beforehand, he is more likely to develop a greater degree of guilt afterward. As mentioned previously, depression generates its own guilt, which is never appropriate and is always exaggerated. It is helpful to be aware of this because guilt further worsens any depression. At times, there may be an initial absence of an appropriate expression of mourning in those who develop depression some months or years later. This may be why friends are concerned when survivors seem unable to cry or verbalize their grief. It is as if the grief can be relieved by its overt expression, and may seem to linger on if buried in the unconscious.

It is important for the physician and the survivor's friends to point out that everything possible had been done for the deceased and that no one should feel guilty. It is also helpful for everyone to anticipate that some degree of inappropriate guilt is common when a close relative dies.

The familial generation of guilt often begins among family members during childhood and may remain latent until disappointment, death, or separation occurs. At that time, unresolved conflicts that had occurred between these relatives may lead to overt depression in the family members. Often, these disagreements relate back to when the child had rejected some of the attitudes and standards of behavior espoused by the parents.

When Frank brought home that little nobody and announced that he was going to marry her, Phyllis wouldn't believe it. After all that she had done for Frank, how could he do such a thing, without even asking her opinion? Phyllis was so disappointed.

That girl wasn't good enough for Frank. She came from a poor background—her parents had not even completed high school. And she wasn't even pretty; just cheap and sexy looking. It had been a big enough disappointment when Phyllis realized that her own marriage was a failure. Her frustration increased when Frank had given up the idea of completing college and becoming a lawyer or a doctor. Phyllis had not felt the reassurance of her son's devotion since he was a little boy. But this was too much. That total stranger would now take Frank away and be his center of attention. It was more than Phyllis could bear. Her initial anger, which in turn caused so much resentment in Frank, gradually turned to guilt and regret. Phyllis felt that she was a total failure as a mother. Frank had not become the success that she knew he was capable of becoming, either in occupation or marriage. And Phyllis felt that somehow it was all her fault, not to have brought him up to behave in what, to her, was a correct manner.

Conflicts of Individuality

The cultural bias to obey parents, even after attainment of adulthood, may be rooted in a misinterpretation of the Biblical commandment to honor parents. To honor and respect them does not necessarily mean to identify with their values and standards of behavior. The first words learned by the child are "good" and "bad" rather than "healthy" or "harmful." The child is normally programmed to be morally opinionated by the bias of his parents' group affiliations in religious, economic, social, political, occupational, and national allegiances.

By the time the child reaches his teens his search for his own individual values and identity usually has caused conflicts with his parents. This conflict is primarily between the role of the obedient child and that of the necessity to be one's own individual self. It is unusual for parents and children to recognize this dilemma and to realize that they can still share love and respect in spite of differences in some of their values. Most parents so closely identify with their children, especially with those of their own sex, that the father cannot accept any differences in values from his son, nor the mother from her daughter. This would be reasonable when the child's differences in values are obviously harmful, such as the use of illegal drugs or other self-destructive habits. But such attitudes as the selection of spouse or the type of occupation, the importance of money and success, political preferences, and the priority of human values are often the main source of conflict and resulting feelings of guilt.

Especially important for parents is to realize that they are apt to be most intolerant of those attitudes and types of behavior in their children that recall the parents' own hang-ups and disappointments. This is especially common in scholastic, occupational, and marital accomplishments. This might explain the frustration of an aggressive businessman who observes that his son is not competitive or hard-driving. Since the father's fear of his own failure is often the driving force behind his own business aggressiveness, he would not be able to accept behavior in his son that be believes would doom the son to failure and would embarrass the father. Similarly, the mother who doesn't consider herself attractive or slim enough is going to generate considerable conflict if her daughter doesn't measure up to the mother's standards of beauty. Both of these examples represent the difficulty in disassociating one's own identity from that of one's child.

Frank had been married for fifteen years, with three children of his own, when he received that late-night phone call that his mother had died of a sudden heart attack. His relationship with his mother had continued to be cool after her initial rejection of his wife, but after he had been married for several months all concerned had gone through the motions of accepting each other. Besides, he had been so busy between his job and trying to spend some time with the kids that he could see his mother only several times a year. Strangely, he now noted a feeling of guilt beginning to grow. And he couldn't understand why he should feel so depressed, when it was his mother who had done the initial rejecting. Nevertheless, after several months of not being himself at work or at home and having a lot of difficulty with sleeping at night, he decided to have his wife make an appointment for him to see their family doctor.

Accepting Personal Advice

Major disappointments that can lead to depression are apt to occur when one deludes one's self into believing that he or she can force others to change their attitudes and behavior. No one can be forced to do anything that he or she does not finally choose to do. One can only suggest or inform. The rest depends on the person who must make the final decision. Even if it appears that someone is being forced to do something that he or she does not want to do, that person has merely chosen one unpleasant alternative in preference to another. Frequently, the more unpleasant alternative would be rejection by someone considered important, such as a parent, spouse, or employer.

It is a paradox that personal advice suggested by one member of a family to another is often met with rejection and anger, while the same advice offered by someone outside the family, such as a physician or minister, does not generate this reaction. The reason for this may be that accepting personal advice may be interpreted as giving up some of one's own individuality. We would prefer that these decisions be our own choice. A family member has such frequent close contacts that he is in a position to repeatedly impose suggestions. An outside professional who has only brief, infrequent contacts does not pose such a threat.

Disappointments with Children

We have been influenced by Freudian psychology to believe that our children's personalities and behavior are almost entirely determined by parental influences during the first five years of life. This overlooks the factors of heredity and outside social influences that continue to be a major factor during the entire period of growing up.

Not all guilt is generated by severe disappointment or major loss. There are many minor everyday regrets that also produce guilt. Most mothers, for instance, experience guilt after yelling at their children, and yet this is a normal, universal way of alleviating everyday tension that occurs in every home. Of course, it can be overdone, but an appropriate amount, short of child abuse, will help prevent a prolonged buildup of resentment. People need to appreciate the normal range of human behavior so that they do not feel guilty over what they have been falsely led to believe is abnormal or undesirable.

The most important attitude to improve the happiness in one's family life is to recognize the importance of individuality in all its members. This awareness will strengthen mutual love, cooperation, and respect. Each member will then be more likely to accept individual responsibility for behavior as it relates to family needs. It is guilt over unresolved conflicts that often prevents people from enjoying family life. It is the same guilt that sets the stage for major depression when inevitable loss through death or separation occurs.

All members of a family should be aware that a certain amount of guilt is bound to occur from inevitable conflicts of values. This is natural and can be controlled by awareness beforehand. Physical closeness, in combination with the emotional openness of family members as they express their deepest feelings, is bound to cause temporary extremes of love and anger. Be prepared to accept this combination of emotions as being unavoidable at times in such a relationship. In this way, the resulting guilt or anger can be handled openly and labeled as the inappropriate but natural imposter that it is.

CHAPTER 11

Dealing with Anger's Distortion of Communication

It was George's calm, silent composure that first attracted Alice. She had been brought up in an atmosphere of continuous loud arguments by her parents, so she wanted a husband who would be agreeable and never show anger. In fact, George resembled, in mannerisms, many of the strong, silent movie stars when westerns were so popular. Even when the movie villain threw a glass of whiskey in the hero's face, the latter didn't even flinch or raise his voice, but quietly knocked out the villain with one punch.

Not that George was a violent sort—just the opposite. He was very quiet and nonargumentative. At a party, he would just sit and listen to the conversation, nodding occasionally in agreement. So what if he didn't say much, it was better than fighting all the time. He'd make a wonderful husband; he was a hard, steady worker, didn't drink excessively, and didn't seem interested in other women. When George asked Alice to marry him, she didn't hesitate to accept.

Anger in Depression

In those depressed people who have little or no guilt, anger is likely to be the major aggravator symptom. Like guilt, anger is a major factor in perpetuating depression, and increases as a result of it. Often anger, guilt, and fear coexist in depression. Anger is, after all, similar to guilt, except that we direct hostility at others rather than ourselves, so it may not seem as initially devastating to our self-esteem. In many depressions it is common for the anger to be suppressed. Prolonged, suppressed anger often results in this hostility

113

being directed back into ourselves. This would explain the frequency of suicide following an emotionally uncontrolled murder. At a more common level, it would explain the frequency of such self-defeating types of behavior as drug or alcohol overindulgence, self-demeaning sexual involvements, or the destruction of cherished personal items that can occur after family disputes. Similarly accountable would be the occurrence of suicide attempts in young people after a major quarrel with a spouse or lover.

Depression is a major cause of persistent hostile behavior. If this were appreciated, it might help reduce the amount of angry response that is returned. This response only aggravates the anger from the hostile person and contributes to the development of the recipient's own anxiety or even depression. On the other hand, some temporary anger is inevitable in everyday life, particularly in the emotional and physical close quarters of family life. The ability to express anger in such a way as not to alienate others is vital to maintaining successful interpersonal relationships. Conversely, the inability to express any anger at all will result in increasing resentment and hostility. This will promote more anxiety and depression and threaten to destroy relationships.

Unloading the Garbage

What results when one family member releases resentment that has been building up toward another can be called "unloading the garbage." It occurs less often outside of the family. This discharge of resentment, which has been building up over a period of time, is often triggered by a minor disagreement, so the emotional tirade usually involves resentments unrelated to the original disagreement. For example, a parent may be discussing his child's coming home too late at night when, without warning, he or she starts yelling that the child's school work has been inadequate, his grooming unsightly, and his general lack of respect unacceptable. Usually this occurs with loud outbursts and loss of emotional control. Often, the person unloading the resentment has been anxious or depressed about other matters unrelated to that particular relationship. Since it is largely a spontaneous, unconscious expression, it is less likely to occur in relationships outside of the family. But when it does occur under these circumstances it is more likely to result from depression. Remember that what is said in the heat of anger is not usually representative of true feelings, as commonly believed, but is a transient product of emotional distortion.

It has been customary to regard chronically angry people as being inherently bad or evil. When we use the expressions "mean bitch" or "mean bastard" there is obviously no sympathy to indicate that these people are usually suffering from the same disease of depression as those who bear great amounts of guilt. The instinctive response to anger is anger. Even when we are aware that anger may be the result of depression, it is difficult to keep from developing anger in return. The automatic basis for the expression of anger has been demonstrated in animal experiments, where electrical stimulation of certain areas of the brain produced stereotyped rage behavior. Who hasn't expressed anger at some time and then felt afterward that he was not able to completely control his rage? Here, chemistry and spontaneous behavior supercede any intellectual reasoning.

Suppression of Anger and Feelings

We have been culturally trained to look upon hostility as a physical threat to the community when, in reality, it is an infrequent occurrence. Our Western religions equate love with good and hate with evil. Children are often raised to suppress feelings of anger when they would actually be appropriate. As a result, many adults are not only unable to express normal anger, but its complement, love, as well. These people are emotionally handicapped. They may get by in occupational and social activities that do not require deep personal involvement, but within their family and married life their robotlike, noncommunicative behavior is totally inadequate. Their lack of both verbal and nonverbal communication of love or anger makes them seem like strangers to their spouses and children. They appear for meals, which are often silently eaten. Then they quietly disappear to the television or newspaper without a word. There is no touching, kissing, and hardly any talking, since it is difficult to do these without evidence of revealing feelings. When an argument does occur, these people often respond with silence and withdrawal. Since the anger is not expressed, it will smolder in resentment. The inability to argue and resolve inevitable differences of opinion will put a major strain on any marriage or family relationship.

After George and Alice had been married for only a few months, Alice began to get concerned. She had bargained for a quiet, agreeable husband, but not for a total stranger. She had not expected the lack of demonstration of his affection and love. Why, he hardly ever touched her. There was no kissing, hugging, or hand-holding. Well, she had heard before how men change after they get married, but she had not anticipated the total lack of conversation in her home. She almost missed hearing the sound of loud yelling that she grew up with; at least you knew there was some life in the house.

Alice was surprised when she began to yell at George for not communicating with her. And the more silent and withdrawn he became in return, the louder and more frequently she yelled at him. They both were miserable, and didn't really know why.

The Strong, Silent Male

Although some women may have difficulty expressing feelings such as love and anger, this problem is much more frequent in men. This is probably due to both biological tendencies and their cultural exaggeration. Even weeks-old infant girls have been shown to make more cooing sounds and respond to voice sounds from adults to a greater extent than do their male counterparts. Culturally, it is appropriate for the female of our species to express deep emotions by the instinctive function of crying. But not for the male.

In fact, the expression of any deep feelings has traditionally been considered unmasculine, especially in our society. This has been well expressed in the ideals evident for many years in the motion picture industry. The male hero has usually been depicted as the strong, silent, unexpressive type. His words are few, the content emotionally understated, and his facial appearance fixed and unexpressive. More recent films, however, have often portrayed men with strong emotions. Women motion picture heroines have revealed their feelings quite openly all along. Actresses have been free to communicate love and hate readily, by word and by nonverbal messages.

The Expressive Female

Returning to the reality of everyday living, while it is common for men to withdraw into silence after an argument with their wives, it is equally common for women to outwardly express their emotions with yelling and crying. Since these tendencies seem to be so strongly rooted in our cultural attitudes, it is wise not to regard them as abnormal as long as they are not too extreme.

The expression "we don't communicate" is an overused, trite phrase commonly used to indicate the inability to express feelings. In reality, this lack of overt dialog is itself a form of communication, usually interpreted by the spouse to mean his or her rejection. While this may be so in some instances, it may also represent the withdrawal and isolation of depression from causes outside of the family. Nevertheless, the resulting apathy or hostility is bound to affect the quality of the marriage and family relationship. It is not reasonable for a husband or wife to become angry with a spouse because he or she is unable to communicate his or her feelings. What should be appreciated is that the person cannot help himself, because of depression or early training. Anger or guilt are not consciously chosen, nor are the resulting impairments in communication. The only way to overcome them is to alleviate the underlying depression.

An established way for many to alleviate depression has been to seek out counseling with a psychologist or psychiatrist. But in those cases where the depressed individual has great difficulty expressing himself or herself, he or she will naturally be reluctant to accept a form of treatment based on verbalizing emotionally charged personal history. Since more men than women have this difficulty in expressing their feelings, it is not surprising that the majority of patients involved in counseling are women; this is not a reliable indication that more women than men are depressed. Men are also more likely to believe that it is a sign of weakness or lack of masculinity to have to seek out help for emotional problems.

When Alice suggested that they both see a marriage counselor, George wouldn't even give a reason for refusing. After Alice had seen a counselor for herself; she began to realize that George's inability to express feelings was a common disorder among American men and was related not only to cultural training, but also to frequently coexisting depression. What she had mistakenly taken to be strong silent composure in George was actually a cover-up for his long-standing anger and depression. The mere fact that she chose him primarily for his inhibitions was an indication of her own distorted priorities. She still loved George and would be willing to put up with his problems, realizing that there was no intention on his part to hurt her feelings. Maybe over the years he might gradually loosen up if she didn't overreact. She certainly couldn't expect him to agree to see a counselor at this time, with his hang-up about communicating.

Cultural bias has equated masculinity with aggressiveness and femininity with passiveness, but this attitude is being gradually revised. There may be some biological and historical basis for these tendencies, since war and hunting have always been traditional male-dominated roles. It may be that the tendency for men to be poor communicators is a result of changes brought about by modern civilization whereby men can no longer express aggressive tendencies in overt action. For some, this repression of aggressive behavior has been interpreted to include all emotional expression and not just anger.

Criminality and Antisocial Personality

When anger results in physical harm to others there is a shift in focus from psychology to law. This cultural compartmentalization of attitudes may be the real reason so little is known about criminality. The polarization of right and wrong behavior into legal and illegal doesn't encourage the objective evaluation of all the degrees between these two extremes. At the same time, it is necessary to protect people from the uncontrolled anger of others as well as from the professional criminal who does his work "in cold blood." The possibility that depression plays a major role in producing the hostility underlying much of criminality would be worth exploring. This might explain why the major spawning ground for crime is in the depressing environment of many inner cities. It would also explain its frequent association with broken homes, alcoholism, and drug addiction, and the frequent history of early abandonment and child abuse by parents that many criminals experience as children. The depressing experience of imprisonment will add to the criminal's attitude that the whole world is against them. Other factors that are also important to criminality are group association and drug usage.

The feelings of anger and worthlessness among criminals promoted by our attitudes reinforce the tendency to depression and violent behavior. At the present time the only system of protection that is available is through the current legal and penal systems and, until something better comes along, these are necessary for public protection.

Many criminals have what is known as an antisocial, or sociopathic, personality. This is designated by early onset, usually before age fifteen, of such antisocial behavior as drug and alcohol abuse; major school behavioral problems; delinquency or illegal acts; persistent lying; unusually early, irresponsible or aggressive sexual behavior; and repeatedly running away from home. In addition, in their adult lives, there are apt to be physical fights and assaults, frequent job changes, unjustified unemployment, illegal occupations, aimless drifting, and criminal acts.

Having both genetic and acquired causes, this poorly understood condition is all the more frustrating to the family because there is often no effective treatment. It is as if antisocial individuals have never developed the usual human capacity to appropriately experience reasonable guilt, and as a result, they overutilize overt hostility and aggression, when others under similar disappointing circumstances might feel sadness, guilt, or repressed anger. In order to maintain the health and preservation of the rest of the family, it may be necessary after trying adequate psychiatric therapy to place young incorrigible individuals in special treatment centers where firm discipline and behavioral modification may sometimes be effective. Recent evidence is accumulating that firm, consistent discipline early in life may help prevent this disorder. Nevertheless, it does seem that the antisocial personality is a type of emotional illness, and like many diseases has many unknown etiologic factors. So it is extremely important for parents and other family members not to assume inappropriate guilt for the behavior of antisocial relatives.

We have noted in this chapter the correlation between the repression of anger, or its inappropriate expression, and the inability to adequately express emotional feelings. These communication problems often are associated with depression, psychosomatic or mental illness, and disruption of work and social or family life. When dealing with family relationships, it is helpful to realize cultural tendencies for men and women to express emotional feelings differently. The tendency for men to withdraw into silence when angry and for women to overtly react when angry should not be regarded as unusual nor necessarily unhealthy by itself, unless it is inappropriately severe or persistent. For the same reasons, women more often utilize overt signs and words of affection than do their mates.

CHAPTER 12

Overcoming Fear of Aging

The trim, muscular, sixty-seven-year-old man had come into the office as a semi-emergency, appearing very upset and worried. He had been examined several months previously and was found to be in excellent health. Not only was he able to work full time, but he swam a half hour daily and walked eighteen holes of golf several times a week. His anxiety attack developed after his wife had repeatedly warned him that he was getting too old to be so active. "Doctor, please tell me," he pleaded, "what I should not do? After all, I am now sixty-seven years old."

No Biologic Year

After asking him, "What exactly is a year?" he answered, "It is the period of time from one birthday to the next."

Almost everyone assumes that a year is a biologic unit of time but it isn't. A year is merely an astronomic unit representing the duration of time that it takes the earth to make one complete revolution around the sun. And no evidence of a biologic clock within our bodies has ever been demonstrated to correlate uniformly with this astronomical year. The individual variation for the onset of puberty varies by years, and the onset of senility, if it develops at all, varies by decades. The most frequently mistaken assumption is that we all change physiologically at the same rate, and further, that this can be measured by the number of birthdays that we have had. Although our existence increases in duration with each birthday, there is a tremendous variation from person to person in the amount of physiologic change. Some seventy-year-olds may be seen playing vigorous tennis, and some poorly conditioned people in their thirties are not even able to walk up three flights of stairs. The frequency of degenerative changes increases statistically as a population grows older, but the individual variation is so great that you cannot depend on age for any individual assessment. Add to this the absence of any precise natural biologic indicators of age and one has the best argument against the irrational, culturally transmitted fear of aging. The popular concept of aging is largely a wastebasket term, filled with exaggeration, bias, and error.

Degenerative Diseases

The greatest misconception equates aging with a number of degenerative diseases that may occur in many older people but can also occur in younger people. The most common of these are arteriosclerosis, cancer, and just the wearing out (atrophy) of an organ due to the disappearance of the active functioning cells. This atrophy may involve the brain even in the absence of arteriosclerosis and is one cause of Alzheimer's disease involving a loss of memory and judgment, but similar atrophy of the brain can be seen in younger people and in some alcoholics.

Mental Slowing

The mental slowing which is most identified with aging is often seen in nursing homes and and similar institutions, yet senility, or Alzheimer's disease, affects but a fraction of those who reach advanced age. Some people are senile as a result of arteriosclerotic strokes, but not all the mental slowing down associated with aging is due to these physical causes. Many cases are due to depression from social isolation and feelings of being useless. Depression among the aged often stems from an attitude of blind cultural bias against age. It has produced one of the greatest social injustices of our times—automatic forced retirement at exactly the same astronomic age—even though people vary by decades in attaining and maintaing efficiency in work capability.

Influencing Factors

Usually it is considered common knowledge that one cannot do anything about aging. On the contrary, there is a great deal that can be done to maintain health and vitality and retard degeneration. One can't alter the contribution from heredity, but regular exercise, such as daily walking, can retard arteriosclerosis and improve mental functioning by increasing circulation and retarding metabolic deterioration. Smoking tobacco hastens hardening of the arteries and lung disease in proportion to the number of packs of cigarettes smoked, as shown in scientific studies. The old saying, "You are what you eat," has been proven right. A healthy diet, low enough in calories to maintain a normal weight—and also low in concentrated sugars and animal fats—has also been proven to be very important for retarding arteriosclerosis. Excessive intake of alcohol or drugs can cause very rapid decline in health and predispose to a large number of diseases.

Perhaps the most important factor of all is one's mental attitude. Maintaining an enthusiastic interest in life, with active participation in activities, is vital. On the other hand, a feeling of uselessness and depression, with withdrawal into physical and mental inactivity, can lead to rapid deterioration, senility, and death.

Retirement

An eighty-year-old related that his physician father used to point out men who had recently retired and predicted that many would be dead within two years. A physician in his eighties who was still working retired because of the expensive premium that was due on his malpractice insurance. Within three weeks he was in a nursing home, unable to recognize the physician who shared his office. This should not be taken to mean that one cannot safely retire, but one needs to develop adequate activities and interests before doing so. The Supreme Court has finally decided that discrimination in employment because of fixed age is as unconstitutional as discrimination because of religion, race, or sex; and those who can demonstrate continued work capacities should not be forced to retire unless they want to. The implications of forced automatic retirement due to a fixed astronomic age go well beyond the emotional and physical harm done to those who would prefer to continue working. We now have a generally accepted assumption in our society that by age sixty-five we are no longer useful, needed, or productive. As a result of age-biased attitudes, fear of aging occurs even in people barely in their twenties. Those societies that pay little attention to age and have no set retirement often have the greatest incidence of longevity and the lowest of so-called senility.

Fear of Aging and Depression

Our youth-favoring and age-rejecting society has resulted in an increased amount of depression about aging not only in the aged, but also in the young, who must look forward to becoming aged.

The awareness of time is even more distorted during depression. Morbid preoccupation persists about past regrets, with feelings of guilt. There is continuing fearful concern regarding future uncertainties, and in severe cases one may even fear the sun rising on a new day after a night of insomnia. Inability to concentrate and work effectively in the present is aggravated by dwelling on fears of the future and regrets for the past.

Loss or morbid distortion of one's sense of humor is a frequent symptom of depression. An essential ingredient of humor—surprise—is based not only on the unexpected and the inappropriate, but also on the use of timing, particularly pausing before relieving the tension of an unexpected conclusion. The ability to maintain a healthy sense of humor has long been recognized as a valuable aid for relieving anxiety and preventing depression.

Present Attentiveness

Our attitudes about time can predispose us to becoming either satisfied or depressed. This dilemma has received a great deal of attention from the ancient Oriental philosophies of Zen and Taoism. These practical psychologies emphasize the importance of becoming more aware of what you are experiencing in the present by practicing greater attentiveness to what you are doing at the time you are doing it. The present is the only time that can be experienced directly by our senses. The past and the future can only be memories or conjecture, even though they are important.

Our daily routine is usually performed so automatically that we are only vaguely aware of what we are doing and of what is going on around us. When we eat, do we fully sense all the smells, sights, and flavors of the food? No. We usually gulp the food down while talking or thinking about something else. When talking with people, are we fully aware of what they are saying, by word or facial expression? The tempo of our modern everyday life induces us to rush through every experience while thinking about something else. Often, this "something else" is an anxiety-filled concern for some future uncertainty or regret-laden past memory. It's no wonder that we lead the world in sales of indigestion aids. One of the most quoted pieces of Zen wisdom simply states, "When you sit, sit; when you eat, eat; when you sleep, sleep."

A rewarding experience will occur when you practice paying more attention to whatever you are doing at the moment you are doing it. You will be amazed at the range and intensity of sensations that had been previously filtered out by inattention and hurrying. A new range of colors, flavors, and inner responses will be experienced from what was previously dull and routine. Everyday activities will become more stimulating. Even usually unpleasant chores may take on some unrealized rewarding aspects or, at the least you might start to learn from them.

A healthy benefit from practicing present attentiveness will, therefore, be a reduction in anxiety and depression. When you are concentrating on what you are doing, you are less likely to dwell on ominous fears of the future or on regretful memories from the past. Another benefit is that learning to concentrate on what you are doing will help you become more efficient and accurate. You will make fewer mistakes, spend less time doing things over, and be happier with the results.

Try a day of practicing present awareness. When you awaken and take a shower, become aware of the texture and temperature of the water in the shower. Taste the full flavor of your breakfast. Look at the trees, clouds, and buildings as you walk to work and sense how they look together as one picture. When listening to someone, concentrate on what he is saying and how he is saying it. This kind of attention-capacity should be helpful for your recreational activities as well as your work.

A major benefit of present awareness will be a fuller enjoyment of all of life's experiences, no matter how menial. This probably is the basis of what is meant by emphasizing the positive aspects of an experience. It does not mean that unpleasant things do not occur; rather, it may mean that by extending our awareness to all aspects of any experience we are likely to discover some of its positive features. Unfortunately, we have been trained by a cynical society to focus mainly on the negative aspects. This attitude may have blinded us from finding these positive aspects. Training ourselves to be more totally aware of the full range of our experiences should help us to become happier and less prone to depression.

Remember that there is no uniform biologic year which measures universal aging; that a year is just a measurement provided by astronomy; that degenerative diseases and mental slowing show such wide individual variations that they should not be presumed to be inevitable; that forced automatic retirement at the same age for everyone is not only based on false assumptions but has been appropriately labeled as unconstitutional; and that healthy habits of nutrition, exercise, and safe use of drugs and alcohol, along with a healthy, active mental attitude, will go a long way to retard degenerative diseases like arteriosclerosis and senility.

The best preparation for the future is a healthy awareness of the present. The skill and effectiveness with which one handles each day's problems will be the basis for effectively managing those in the future. The transition from one era to another does not occur abruptly—it changes gradually from day to day. Present attentiveness will help keep you on top of these gradual changes. Since fear of aging is so closely related to the ultimate fear, the next chapter explores this rarely discussed subject, as well as the necessary emotions to overcome it—faith, hope, and meaning for life.

CHAPTER 13

Overcoming the Ultimate Fear

The first real sense of how it feels to be depressed often occurs when, as small children, we first realize that our total existence—all sensations, awareness, and communication with loved ones—will someday cease to be. This inherent fear of death may be the primary source for all the anxiety and depression that will occur during our lives. Freud may have erred when he suggested that sexual frustration (rather than fear of death) was the main cause of neurosis. By adulthood, the fear of death has usually been repressed into our unconscious to provide a wide variety of disguised symptoms and other fears. Fear of flying may simply be fear of dying.

Religious Concepts

In order to provide relief from anxiety about death, most societies have devised religious theories that are presented as fact. These vary from the Oriental concept of continuous recycling through new human or animal lives, to the Western concept of eternal perpetuation of the intact personality, or soul. And the more choice relocations in either case are to go to those with the most moral prior lives. The main force for the development of religious systems was probably the need to relieve anxiety from such basic but puzzling life problems as death, disease, and aging. The biggest puzzle of all remains the phenomenon of death. This probably underlies the universal need for faith, hope, and meaning for life, since total loss of some sort of continuity after death would seem to nullify any real meaning to existence.

126

Realistic Miracles

These statements should not be taken to indicate our rejection of a concept of a supreme organizing force. True miracles do occur every moment of every day, everywhere. It is not the possible rare suspension of the laws of nature that is the real miracle. It is the mathematical consistency with which these natural laws operate throughout the universe that compels one to believe in such an organizing force. The development of the human mind is the biggest miracle of all. That we have some slight understanding of natural phenomenon does not detract from the miracle of life and nature. Even though this means that we cannot honestly assume anything more specific than the existence of a supreme organizer, it is still assuring.

One law of physics is the conservation of matter and energy. This states that nothing can be created or destroyed, but can only be changed from one form to another. For example, when wood burns, the solid carbon it contains is changed to carbon dioxide gas, which is invisible. This concept might be applied to the individual self: after death, there is no destruction but only an unknown change. It seems inconceivable that a force that shuns destruction of molecules and atoms would allow destruction of the most intricate achievement ever accomplished—that of the individual human mind.

Need for Faith—a Nonreligious Definition

We come to the necessity of some sort of faith to maintain happiness and prevent depression. A broad definition of faith, not restricted to religion, by the late Paul Tillich, a prominent theologian, includes three criteria: first, faith includes a sense of vital ultimate concern that occupies a central, important position in one's life; second, faith makes significant demands for one's unselfish commitment; and finally, it offers an ultimate promise of great rewards. It seems apparent that this definition of faith can apply to any system of beliefs, institutions, or people and can include religions, science, political parties, social philosophies, and occupations. This explains the sacrificial religious fervor that can be seen in nationalism, revolutionary movements, labor unions, charismatic leaders, and in lovers.

There is obviously a faith relationship when people marry. They start out totally committed, have great expectations about their relationship and are prepared to unselfishly devote their entire lives to each other. As might be expected, this level of faith may be difficult for many to live up to and is the reason for the bitterness that often follows an unhappy marriage.

Man, indeed, does not live by bread alone. People need relationships based on faith to maintain their hopes, enthusiasm, and direction. A frequent symptom of depression is a total loss of faith and hope, so that life no longer has meaning or purpose. Faith and hope are oriented to the future, with expectations of rewards from today's hard work and sacrifice. No wonder such great disappointment can occur when we encounter divorce, disappointment with children, and disillusionment with organized religion or political systems. Relationships based on some sort of faith have been universally necessary to give life meaning and purpose. For healthy motivation and zest for living, it is essential to seek out those faith relationships that are most likely to offer long-term satisfaction based on appropriate individual values.

The fact that temporary loss of faith, hope, and meaning occurs in depression establishes that these are not just superficial values but are necessities. Some sort of faith relationship is required by everyone, whether religiously pious or strongly atheistic. It would be grossly negligent to avoid a discussion of religion in any book on anxiety and depression, since this is where most of our cultural involvement with faith, hope, and meaning has traditionally been concentrated.

Influence of Religion

Many of the conscious and social symptoms of depression deal with attitudes that are greatly influenced by religious training. These include—in addition to faith, hope, and meaning—guilt, anger, fear, reduction in self-image, despair, futility, attitudes toward suicide, loneliness, and responsibility to others. The social symptoms of hostility, jealousy, and seclusiveness, along with the frequent associated problems of alcoholism, drug dependency, marital infidelity, or antisocial behavior are a prime concern of most religions. This does not mean to imply that religion or its rejection has either increased or decreased the incidence of depression. Like so many other influences, it has to be evaluated on an individual basis. Undoubtedly, many individuals have maintained lifelong security from their beliefs and faith. On the other hand, there are those whose guilt and self-rejection stem from religious ideals that they cannot live up to.

Perhaps the greatest confusion has arisen from the occasional hypocrisy that has involved religion, like any other man-made institution. It's hard to accept religion as just an earthly institution because of its unusually high standards of morality, the sacrifice and dedication of its clergymen, and the altruistic purposes for which it was conceived. Since these organizations are composed of mortal human beings, it is unavoidable that from time to time some of its leaders may have been corrupted by their power.

Faith in a Supreme Being or Faith in Religion?

It is important not to confuse faith in God with faith in religion. Another important distinction that will help prevent disillusionment and loss of faith is to differentiate the practical wisdom of the original religious philosophers from the political religious organizations that developed in their name, often many years after the founders died. For example, Dostoevski wrote a story in which Jesus came back to earth at the time of the Spanish Inquisition and was immediately condemned to death for his anti-Christian attitudes. The worldly wisdom of the founding religious philosophers has been diluted by attention to the life history and personality of the founders, with the resulting concentration mainly on ritual rather than the conscious search for meaning and application to current living. Of course, there is also a need for meaningful ritual. Religion is further compartmentalized by confining religious activities to special buildings and certain days of the calendar. There are individual and group exceptions, of course, but the tendency of many to isolate religious roles and values from other kinds can predispose to inner conflicts.

Whether or not one has ties with any particular religion, it is how this relationship affects one's sense of individuality that will influence emotional health. Ideally, religion should unify all of life's experiences into a meaningful whole, allowing the individual a sense of consistency and identification in all his various roles and values. On the other hand, when a person separates his religious life and values from his other priorities, he is likely to suffer from conflicts of values.

Even without religious beliefs, one still needs some sort of relationship based on faith in order to survive emotional stress. That faith may not only be necessary for psychological survival but for physical survival as well was demonstrated repeatedly in the concentration camps during World War II. Those who just gave up and lost all hope often died shortly thereafter, while those who maintained some sort of faith and hope were most likely to survive.

We must no longer allow fear of death, the ultimate human concern, to be repressed into the reservoir from which so much anxiety and depression arises. Faith, hope, and meaning for life cannot be ignored as only a Sunday School concern, but must be understood as a major psychological need, whose loss almost always occurs during depression.

Faith itself must be understood for its nonreligious meaning as the binding emotion for all committed relationships: in marriage, political affiliations, occupations, social and family relationships, committed ways of life, and even toward science itself.

Those who feel that science and belief in a supreme organizing force are incompatible with each other need only to realize the unbelievable mathematical consistency of the natural laws of physics, chemistry, and biology.

CHAPTER 14

Preventing a Depressed Marriage

Disappointment in love expectations is inevitable when there is confusion between the meaning of love as an ideal sexual experience in contrast to love as a totally committed faith relationship. Since isolated sex-love without commitment tends to be transient, superficial, self-serving, and fractionated, it usually focuses only on certain parts of the body rather than on one's whole individuality. Although very intense for brief periods, isolated sex-love tends to be of only limited longevity, and easily succumbs to apathy and boredom.

Faith-Love

In contrast to isolated sex-love, faith-love requires mutual respect, kindness, and commitment by both partners to a meaningful, long-term exclusive relationship based on the meaning of faith. This involves deep mutual concern for each other's total individuality, including both mind and body. The specialness of this faith-love commitment is such that both its faith-love and sex-love aspects are exclusive to only one partner for the duration of that relationship. The fallacy that you can love everybody occurs because of confusion between the need for commitment in faith-love and the lack of it in isolated sex-love. Although one can try to like everybody, by definition of specialness it is impossible to really love everybody.

The selfish, transient nature of isolated sex-love without faith-love predisposes to depression because it lacks the security of faith for the future and ultimate meaning for the relationship. Frantic desperation underlies trying one meaningless, dehumanizing sexual encounter after another in an attempt to find happiness, and ends up aggravating the underlying depression. In recent years, increased preoccupation with sexuality (sex-love) without faith-love has been associated with a staggering increase in divorce and depression. The best evidence for the almost universal need for an exclusive long-term combined faith-love and sex-love relationship is the overwhelming frequency with which the bitterness of divorce is subsequently followed by the willingness to try marriage again.

Combined Sex- and Faith-Love

This does not diminish the importance of a satisfying sex-love to a faith-love relationship. Sexual dissatisfaction may be both a cause and a result of an ailing faith-love. Furthermore, even the tendency to pass judgment on a partner's sexual performance, especially in a critical manner, is often an indication of dissatisfaction with the whole faith- and sex-love relationship. The tendency for a happy combined faith- and sex-love is not to judge nor to compare sexual performance, but to appreciate it as part of a multidimensional, whole relationship. In this way, faith-love is usually a positive, dominant influence on one's attitude toward sex-love.

Selecting a Mate

Making the decision regarding which person to share one's life with is usually the single most important decision one will ever make. This is because of the prolonged, intimate sharing of unconscious emotional feelings and behavior. Since both depression and optimism are communicable, one's potential for happiness is therefore most greatly influenced by the mate's emotional status. As important as occupational stresses can be, they nevertheless are confined only to the superficial degrees of emotional involvement found in business or work relationships. With the exception of compulsive overworkers, the dissolving of a work relationship does not usually approach in magnitude the emotional repercussion of a dissolution of a combined faith- and sex-love relationship.

The best time to make any major decision is when you don't have to. This is because you will then be making that decision on the positive factors of the merits of the situation. For instance, if you decide to buy a house when you don't have the negative pressure of being forced out of your present residence, you are more likely to find what you will continue to enjoy, and less likely to be stuck with something obtained in desperation. Similarly, you are more likely to be disappointed when you select a new mate at a time when you are desperate to escape from another or from an unpleasant parental home situation.

The novelty effect of becoming involved in a love relationship mainly for its stimulation from the boredom of depression is more apt to center around the superficial transciency of isolated sex-love rather than the deeper faith-love relationship. Emphasis on novelty may also predispose some to experiment with unhealthy sexual alternative life-styles. On the other hand, when the stimulation of a new sex-love relationship is combined with the compatibility of individualities to allow for faith-love also, the original novelty effect can be replaced by a stable relationship.

Effect of Depression

The recent epidemic of marriage failure and divorce must be related to common influences that have arisen in our society. One key factor has been the frequency of depression in the past decade. Associated with depression have been increases in the incidence of unfaithfulness, alcoholism, and drug abuse, which further aggravate marital relationships. Depression impairs the ability to relate and communicate with loved ones: one may be able to hide deep feelings from friends and co-workers, but at home emotions are spontaneous. Hostility and inappropriate anger often result from unrecognized depression, which is bound to strain any relationship. Depression and anxiety are communicable, and repeated exposures to these emotions tend to affect people closely involved.

The effect of anxiety or depression is most often to decrease sexual interest or capacities. Occasionally these conditions will lead to increased sexual activity, especially with new partners. Depression, therefore, is a common cause for a previously stable individual to withdraw from a marriage commitment, or to seek out promiscuous or extramarital affairs. The most important practical point is that when a partner ceases to function in a sexual capacity, it does not necessarily mean a rejection of the other partner, since it may occur as a result of depression or anxiety due to factors outside of their relationship. In our medical experience, occupational tensions for the man and familial tensions for the woman bring this about most often. Unfortunately, impotence or frigidity are often falsely regarded as conscious antagonistic behavior by the other partner and will threaten their relationship. Emotional conflict between the couple may be the primary factor, but often outside influences first bring about these tensions.

Depression will often exaggerate the tendency to have two

different personalities, so when two individuals live together, they may really be sharing four personalities. The unconscious, uninhibited behavior pattern released in the intimacy of the home is rarely seen by outsiders. Home is where fears and angers are kept, and home is where they are usually released. Since we all have tension, it is helpful to anticipate that two personalities may emerge from time to time in the individuals with whom one will share his or her life. It is important to be able to detect a sick unconscious mind before committing oneself to a long-term relationship. This can usually be detected during the courting period, as inappropriate outbursts of violent or hostile behavior, drug or alcohol dependency, or marked withdrawal and inability to communicate. Distorted attitudes that seem bizarre may be another symptom of a disordered mind.

It may be revealing to literally interpret the words used to express the quality of a love relationship. To be "madly in love" may truly describe the insanity or inappropriateness of the relationship, or as emphasis on raw sensation without reason. The fact that sexual activities can be used in the context of hate and anger, as in rape, is evidence that sex-love can at times be sex-hate. But faith-love, as long as it endures, cannot be maintained in the presence of prolonged hate and anger, although it readily absorbs the necessary transient conflicts that are bound to occur in any close relationship.

Balancing Commitment with Individuality

The unique challenge for a happy marriage is to balance commitment with individuality. At first glance these goals might appear to be in conflict, since commitment would seem to require surrender of the freedom to seek out other faith- and sex-love relationships; however, the fulfillment of individuality and freedom requires accepting responsibility for behavior agreed upon beforehand, when the couple pledged themselves to each other. Any faith relationship is characterized by ultimate concern for the object of that faith (in this case the spouse), the willingness to sacrifice and devote effort (for his or her behalf), and the expectation of great satisfaction or happiness in return. Naturally, there are bound to be human limitations in the completeness of living up to these expectations, and some disappointment is inevitable, but to the extent of its sincerity, this commitment provides the determination to overcome such obstacles as unhealthy fads, emotional or physical illness, financial difficulties, problems with relatives, and numerous other disappointments.

The main problem that can result from long-term commitment without adequate stimulation is boredom from lack of variety. Therefore, to balance commitment with this sense of variety requires the full appreciation of each other's individuality. Compatible differences in each other's personality, attitudes, and behavior will allow sufficient variety and challenge to provide stimulation and even occasional necessary confrontations. This is a delicate balance: to have enough differences to allow for adequate variety but at the same time not to have such great differences as to cause continual or severe conflicts.

The key to this balance is the sharing of similar attitudes and standards of behavior about activities that are engaged in by the couple together. These shared values include the type of home, social and material goals, expectations regarding children and general life-style. These compatibilities must be determined before deciding whether to marry.

Attitudes and standards of behavior that the couple need not share are those regarding individual activities that can be engaged in without threat to the relationship. These can include such activities as reading, hobbies, sports, and educational interests. Different values regarding philosophical, religious, and political preferences are more apt to cause problems if the couple is actively involved and strongly identified with opposing viewpoints. On the other hand, if either of the individuals are relatively indifferent toward these beliefs, there is less likely to be significant conflict.

Compatibility of Temperaments

A most important compatibility difference involves individual temperaments. One could imagine either the boredom or extreme conflict that could result if he or she were married to someone with exactly the same temperament. Most couples need an occasional argument to ventilate inevitable emotional stresses. If both mates are so passive as to never voice a conflicting opinion, the resulting boredom and repressed anger can be very destructive to the relationship, but on the other hand, if both are highly volatile and prone to become easily upset, the constant fighting can be similarly disruptive. It therefore requires compatible differences in temperament to find the moderate variety needed for a stimulating but not explosive relationship.

While depression imposes a stress on any marriage, reasonable differences of mood can be complementary. The overly enthusiastic person who is apt to undertake more than he can handle can be balanced by a spouse who is more cautious and not so carefree; therefore, some individual differences in personalities are necessary for a satisfying relationship, while other categories require similarities for the relationship to be healthy.

Emphasizing Marital Roles

A paradoxical change often occurs in the couple's attitudes and behavior toward each other when they undergo the transition from lovers to being officially married. This unfortunate change occurs mainly in those who are most prone to rigidly follow group role behavior, rather than maintain their own individual attitudes. They forget the major reason why, as lovers, they were so happy with each other—they were primarily concerned with each other as individuals, rather than cast in the rigid group role interpretations of husband and wife. Emphasizing roles destroys the attractiveness and stimulation that individuality encourages. For example, if you emphasize that the most important function for the husband is to be a wage earner while the most important role for the wife is to keep a neat house, you are bound to lose respect for those individual values that were responsible for bringing you together in the first place. From emphasizing roles comes the disastrous change in attitude from "What more can I do for my lover?" to "What my spouse is supposed to do for me."

The vast majority of people do need the security of the commitment of marriage, but they do not need to change their emphasis from individual priorities to group roles. A couple can still have a reasonably neat home and reasonable success in occupation without giving these a priority over human individual values. These routine, but necessary, role aspects of marriage can be done quietly, without making them the center of attention.

Outside Influences

The ability of a couple to happily share reasonable mutual dependency and trust depends upon their ability to be relatively independent of outside influences such as fads, media-promoted values, unhealthy group loyalties and other common influences. As discussed earlier in this chapter, there is a need for both diversity and sharing within the marital relationship, but ignoring the essential faith- and sex-love commitment necessary for marriage sets the stage for its own destruction. Most happy marriage relationships are obtained by those who maintain their full faith- and sex-love commitments by preventing outside intrusions, not by seeking them out. We have called this the "private marriage" concept. It requires the awareness of the most frequent disruptive influences on the marriage relationship. This way, the couple can mutually determine beforehand which standards of behavior are more likely to cause subsequent major problems. Once major conflict occurs, emotional overreaction interferes with reasonable cooperation. This anticipation of major problem areas allows preventive insulation from these outside factors, but not isolation. Just the opposite—it requires the couple to be totally aware of all influences, to be prepared for all possible marital problems.

Five of the most common perennial marital influences are the parents-in-law, the friends of the couple, their occupations, organizations and groups, and their own children. While these five influences have always been present, the recent almost epidemic acceleration of divorce and marriage failure have occurred in association with rapid changes regarding all traditional faith relationships such as in religion, government, and education, as well as in the family.

The In-Laws

The relationship to the parents-in-law involves such a sensitive area that the couple may not even be able to discuss it for months or years. At the heart of the problem is the need to transfer the primary dependency from the parents to the new mate, which requires a reshuffling of priorities.

Changes in role are understandably difficult for the parents. They have spent the lifetime of the child responding to his or her physical and emotional needs, now some stranger will take that number one position.

What about the feelings of the young couple toward their parents-in-law? They also feel uncomfortable trying to force themselves to act like a close relative to someone who is also like a stranger. Although the couple may have great love for each other, this does not automatically transfer to the in-laws. The emotional ties of the spouse to his or her own parents are usually such that the other spouse often feels the need to pretend a closeness that isn't sincere. Even before the marriage, the wedding plans usually require so many compromises between the two families that there are often hurt feelings from the start.

Actually there is no reason why the young couple and their in-laws cannot be comfortable with each other if they are all aware that this rivalry is normal in our culture and, therefore, no one is to blame—and that this transfer of dependency is a necessary but difficult adjustment.

Since guilt and anger can develop from these in-law frustrations, they can form the basis for the development of a depression that could erode marital happiness. It need not occur if the couple realistically anticipate the problem and they mutually decide on how to handle it. Their attitudes to their in-laws could then be more relaxed, and they could avoid the hostility that occurs from suppressed or dishonest feelings.

Transference of dependency can be facilitated if the young couple demonstrate their capabilities by making as many of their own major decisions as possible and taking care of their own responsibilities. This requires not only reasonable financial independence but also not involving the parents-in-law in the private affairs of the couple. This includes such areas as arguments, sex problems, child-rearing, financial problems, or general life-style. It does not preclude seeking opinions from parents-in-law in areas that both mates mutually agree to beforehand; but the final decisions should still be left to the young couple.

Friends and Privacy

A second major perennial influence that can erode marital happiness is overinvolvement with friends. This does not mean that friendships are not needed for a balanced life, but that a necessary amount of privacy can be lost through overdependency upon friends. A reasonable amount of privacy is necessary to preserve the couple's own special faith-love relationship.

This essential privacy of the couple can be lost by devoting all their recreational time to being with others. Custom often prevents the couple from communicating with each other when they are with friends on a social occasion. Even the seating arrangements at dinner parties usually separate them. Often the only conversation between the couple during the week is related to problem-solving about the household, children, finances, and occupation. These discussions occur in an unromantic environment of hurry in the morning and fatigue at night. That is in contrast to conversation with a friend of the opposite sex at a weekend party, where both are groomed and dressed to the peak of attractiveness and the talk only about pleasant, stimulating topics. In order to maintain some romance in their marriage, it is necessary for the couple to reserve time to enjoy themselves without friends, relatives or children. This still leaves other times to go out with friends and relatives. It is also beneficial for the couple to vacation by themselves occasionally if at all possible. In our overcommitted schedules, the lowest priority is usually allotted to time for the couple to spend by themselves.

Too much time and closeness between two couples may occassionally lead to extramarital liaisons. Overexposure to the depressing problems of friends can also cause anxiety and depression in the listener.

Occupational Influences

Problems relating to the husband's or wife's occupation are bound to spill over into the marriage at times. This can be minimized if the upset spouse explains that it is work tension and not dissatisfaction with the spouse that is the cause. Extra work hours are also inevitable. but should not be allowed to continue indefinitely because of the resulting overload anxiety-depression state that will be a strain on both spouses. Some wives may be content to make their homes and their families their sole occupation, while others will find a need for outside involvement, such as a job. The key to the situation is for them to make this decision on the basis of their own needs, balanced with those of their families. A frequent solution is part-time work, volunteer activities, or taking some course of study. Although it is often boring to be confined to the house full-time, it is usually unrealistic to expect a job to continue to be exciting once the novelty has worn off. In many cases, outside work is necessary for financial needs or for luxuries that have become necessities. Occupation can also serve as an excuse to prevent or delay having children when one spouse desires them and the other does not.

For most husbands and wives, working together full-time will make it more difficult to maintain a happy marriage. Although there are exceptions, the attitudes and behavior of spouse and lover are often at odds with those of a competitive co-worker or obedient employee. Too much togetherness can also be a stress. Many secretaries who marry the boss find that, after marriage, they are unable to continue that job, but part-time working together may not be difficult for some couples.

Working with any relative often causes problems. The hostility that often develops when a son goes into his father's business has given rise to the organization called SOBS, "Sons of Bosses." The ambition of the young man to fully take charge is often frustrated by the reluctance of the older man to give up his authority and sense of importance. The daughter-in-law then faces the problem of the usual discomfort with her in-laws, now complicated by financial dependence on them. When brothers and sisters go into a family business, the situation is often marked with jealousy and rivalry. If one must work with relatives, he or she must be prepared to deal with these problems.

A major adjustment will be required when the husband retires and the couple spend most of their time together. Too much togetherness may be aggravated by the frequency of boredom and depression in a formerly working spouse, who misses having regular employment. This may be prevented by the development of outside hobbies and interests before retirement.

Groups and Organizations

Overcommitment to outside responsibilities may lead to an overload depression that endangers the happiness of a marriage. Housewives are particularly vulnerable because being a homemaker is not generally considered the full-time job that it is. It is difficult to say no when someone is asked to volunteer for too many organizations. There is often a distortion of values in which the group is considered more important than the family. The husband can also overextend himself at work and in outside involvements.

Modern life has become increasingly dominated by a mushrooming number of groups and organizations for every aspect of life. Whether they be political, social, educational, religious, or recreational, there are special interest values that are usually promoted. Problems arise when group attitudes and loyalties are in conflict with those of the married couple. Groups also compete for time that the couple could otherwise spend together. They may also promote conflicts in attitudes between the couple, such as those held by an exclusive social club or a polarized political group. Many people are not even aware that they are following group attitudes that often do not reflect the way they really feel when they are alone. It is important for the couple to anticipate which group might be the most threatening to their relationship and to find those that are appropriate. A balance could be developed between groups that are shared by the couple and those which each can belong to separately.

Children

Most couples will require several years to really know each other well before they can adjust to the loss of privacy as a result of having children. Although some couples will decide never to have children, most couples will desire them. The need to procreate is strongly rooted in human instinct, beyond the need of sex alone. Recently there have been more social options as to when, or if, to have children. It is important for the couple to agree before marriage whether or not to have children, since this disagreement later might be catastrophic.

The most difficult idea to accept is that children are not duplicates of ourselves, even though they may resemble us physically. The best evidence that they are unique individuals is that most siblings differ in personality and temperament from each other, yet they have the same parents. (Once it is accepted that children are the unique individuals they are, parents will not be so upset when children's hangups remind them of their own!)

There is no book, organization, or authority that can tell parents how to raise their children. Basically it's not an intellectual exercise, but deep unconscious feelings that are involved. Appropriate suggestions from experts may be helpful at times but, for the most part, it's an intuitive process of on-the-job learning.

Divorce

Like the use of war to solve group conflicts, the use of divorce almost always causes casualties of its own in the form of depression among all members of the family. While divorce is occasionally necessary to solve an incurable marriage incompatibility (psychological or physical), the dramatic increase in this means of solving marital problems strongly suggests that it is being overutilized due to social imitations and faddism. Even marriage counselors and other professionals often dangle the divorce solution as an immediate means of solving marriage problems. Books and television programs dealing with divorce sometimes start out by saying, "Assuming that you have made the decision to divorce," rather than encouraging an evaluation of its appropriateness. It has almost become romanticized with terms like "creative divorce" and suggestions of new sexual fulfillment. The reality of divorce, like war, is usually that it's hell.

To be sure, divorce does have its place to relieve the unsolvable chronic depressions that can occur, as from persistent infidelity, chronic alcohol and drug abuse, sadistic hostility, or other manifestations of chronic severe personality disorders. But such currently popular reasons for divorce as, "He (or she) has not grown with me," "We don't communicate," or "She's not willing to try those new sexual techniques described in the latest best-sellers," confirm the currently selfish attitudes being promoted not only by the media but even by professionally qualified experts in counseling. Of course, there is bound to be impairment in communication when either one of the couple is depressed. It is only selfish fantasy to assume that a spouse has not grown because he or she does not adopt new fad attitudes and standards of behavior that the other spouse has chosen to follow.

Most importantly, the basic premise of faith-love is to value the total individuality of the spouse, not out of selfish possessiveness but out of the admiration and devotion that led to one's commitment in the first place. No one forces you to marry a particular individual. You chose to do so out of free will. If you decide later that it was an inappropriate decision born out of immaturity, how do you know now that your current decision to seek divorce is appropriate and mature? This is a question that only you can answer.

The basic questions to be considered as to whether or not divorce is the answer are: Is the treatment worse than the disease? Will you be happier and emotionally more healthy once the post-divorce depression is over, or will you regret the decision and be more depressed than you were before the divorce? Will the divorce really solve your depression, or are you really depressed because of personal or outside problems that have only secondarily affected your marriage?

Impairment in communication, dissatisfaction, and hostility are usually taken to mean personal rejection of one's spouse when, in reality, these are often impersonal manifestations of the disease of depression, so destroying a marriage that may be the victim rather than the cause of this disease is unlikely to bring relief.

Prior to the past two decades, divorce was usually only a last resort. Since most depressions eventually were cured (with or without treatment) within six months to two years, the marriage relationship could often become satisfactory again. Now, with social pressure to seek a prompt solution by divorce, there are bound to be many marriages that would have become healthy again if not prematurely destroyed. It is very helpful to seek out a wise counselor to help determine whether the marriage itself is the cause of the depressing situation or merely its victim, so that appropriate individual treatment could be applied or, when really necessary, divorce could be utilized appropriately. Not all counselors are above social fad and imitation. When divorce is recommended before adequate evaluation, especially when the couple really want to stay together, a second opinion from a different counselor may be necessary.

As to who can fulfill the role of counselor, this includes psychologists, psychiatrists, marriage and family counselors, ministers, interested physicians, psychiatric social workers, or any of a wide variety of trained or, in some states, relatively untrained people who may be free to call themselves marriage counselors.

Except by reputation from other clients or referral from a physician, it is difficult to select an appropriate marriage counselor by oneself. Unfortunately, these professionals are often sought out only after the faith-love securing the marriage has been irreversibly destroyed. Like any other faith, once it is gone it is difficult to re-establish. It is far better to seek out counseling earlier, when threatening marital conflicts are beginning to become a repetitious habit. Some couples even seek out premarital counseling in the hope of anticipating how to handle major problems before they occur.

It has become fashionable not to consider the effects of divorce on children. This is justified by the current belief that it is just as traumatic for the children to be exposed to continuous marital conflict between the parents as it is for them to experience the trauma of divorce. Like most unproven generalizations, this one needs to take into consideration the severity of the marital conflicts, the individual needs of different children, and the appropriateness of the divorce solution. It seems apparent that such unrestricted generalizations are created to fill a need for justifying social trends. In this case, it gives permission for a divorce-prone society to ignore responsibility for the individual needs of the children.

The emotional depression that follows divorce is not unlike that which follows the death of a loved one. It affects all members of the family—husband, wife, and children—and the guilt, anger, and sadness is much like mourning the death of the marriage. Nevertheless, when divorce is appropriately necessary, the ill effects on the family may still be less than the ill effects from an incurably sick marriage.

CHAPTER 15

Psychometabolic Rhythms and Seasonal Affective Disorder

It seems appropriate that the last chapter of this book, dealing as it does with natural cycles and rhythms (not to be confused with biorhythms), suggests that existence cannot be explained as just a finite linear phenomenon with an absolute beginning and end, but must involve continuity through repetition of similar forms and behavior. Biologically, the genetic potentials cycled through our ancestors contain chemical messages whose origins must go back at least to our beginnings to be able to reproduce similar human forms.

The previous chapters have attempted to offer the reader practical advice on how to avoid anxiety and depression in today's world, or how to cope with them if avoidance has not been possible. We now wish to turn to a subject that is more speculative and technical than the material elsewhere in this book. In doing so, we introduce innovative concepts based on personal clinical experience in combination with information from research literature. It is hoped that other professionals will be encouraged to evaluate these themes, so that they can be either developed or refuted. AIn the meantime, these concepts can serve to help everyone understand the underlying metabolic basis for emotional reactions.

Sunlight and Darkness

Of all the natural rhythms influencing living behavior, the daily cycle of sunlight and darkness is the most dynamic. In synchrony with the twenty-four-hour rotation of the earth, most animals, including humans, display their greatest activity and energy during the daytime presence of sunlight, and have their peak inactivity, culminating in sleep, during the hours of darkness. This dependence on the sun for vitality, visibility, warmth, availability of food, and sense of security has been universally recognized, as evidenced by its frequent use as a symbol for God in many ancient pagan religions and its high priority of creation in the second sentence of the Bible, right after the heavens and the earth.

The emotional effects of sunlight are evident in the folk wisdom of everyday language. A sunny, bright disposition signifies happiness while a dark, brooding one indicates sadness. Sunrises and sunsets have long served as powerful emotional inspirations for poetry, music, and religion.

Jet lag is a temporary disturbance simulating an emotional disorder that occurs in many people as a result of sudden loss or gain in time zones after east-west or west-east jet travel.

Since this syndrome consists of fatigue, irritability, difficulty in concentration, sleep disturbance, and digestive disturbance, it is similar to a transient anxiety-depression state. Since it doesn't occur in north-south jet travel, the cause must therefore be the sudden loss or gain in the amount of daylight per twenty-four-hour cycle. This disrupts the normally synchronized functionings of a variety of physiologic processes such as those involving sleep, energy, digestion, mood, and intellectual ability.

The emotional effects of cyclic seasonal changes may involve more than the obvious influences of temperature change and inclement weather. Even in moderate climates where weather remains mild the year round, there are peak incidences of depression, serious illness, and arteriosclerotic deaths during the winter. Other seasonal factors can be reduction in the amounts of outdoor recreation and exercise available because of shorter or stormier days, and seasonal holiday reminders recalling sadness or loneliness from family loss or disappointment.

In addition to these seasonal sentimental and weather influences, we believe that the seasonal shortening and lengthening of sunlight may also have a direct physiologic influence upon health, mood, and energy. Textbooks in medicine have long questioned why there are peak incidences of peptic ulcer in spring and fall. Since these are the seasons of greatest accelerated change in ratio of daily sunlight to darkness, it seems reasonable to speculate that an illness known to arise from problems of psychological adjustment might be directly affected by biochemical adjustments to rapid seasonal changes in the durations of sunlight.

Similarly, peak hospitalization rates for severe endogenous depression, suicides, and alcoholism also occur in the spring and fall, even though the greatest overall incidence of reactive depression seems to occur in winter. We suspect this apparent discrepancy is related to the differences in origin of the two main types of depression. The usually more severe endogenous depression, which is more likely to require hospitalization, seems to arise spontaneously from internalized bodily chemical factors while the usually less severe reactive depressions have obvious external precipitating psychological stresses preceding their onset. It seems reasonable to speculate that the rapid changes in ratio of light to darkness that occur in the spring and the fall might act directly as a physical-chemical influence upon those whose depression is thought to be more physically endogenous in origin.

In fact, the famous French sociologist, Emile Durkheim, established that suicide rates were highest in the spring and fall when seasonal changes in duration of sunlight were greatest, and the rates increased eightfold as one moved from less polar to more polar latitudes where these sunlight duration variations are more extreme. Nevertheless, he did not recognize a cause-and-effect relationship.

Seasonal Affective Disorder

Seasonal changes in the amounts of light and darkness have now been recognized as causing a special type of depression known as "seasonal affective disorder," or SAD. It has the same symptoms as other forms of depression but tends to recur every fall or winter.

For this disorder the use of very bright lights in special experimental settings has met with with some success as have standard treatments with medication and counseling.

The Pineal Gland

After decades of personally searching for some physiologic explanation by which to understand how biologic circadian rhythms are integrated to alternating sunlight and darkness, I was gratified to learn of a scientific discovery that may have answered this question. The pineal gland, buried deep within the center of the brain and less than the size of a pea, is now known to secrete a unique hormone, melatonin, directly under the stimulation of darkness, and is turned off enzymatically by the presence of artificial or natural sunlight. Derived from serotonin by a specific enzyme found only in the pineal, melatonin acts upon the nearby hypothalamus and brain stem to synchronize its twenty-four-hour circadian influence upon the master pituitary gland and hypothalmic centers for all the organs and endocrine glands of the body. At the same time, melatonin has been shown to promote normal sleep, regulate the timing of puberty, and to be necessary for healthy emotional behavior.

This amazing pineal is also unique in that it has no direct nerve connections with the brain that surrounds it, It receives its only nerve fiber stimulation from outside the brain through the sympathetic cervical ganglion nerve center located in the neck. This in turn receives its special nerve fibers from the retinas of the eyes, where light stimulation acts to turn off the enzyme that makes melatonin in the pineal. Anatomically and physiologically, it would appear that the pineal is primarily programmed to be influenced by external factors of light and darkness rather than by other parts of the brain, although such factors as cold temperature and stress also can affect it. The philosopher Descartes may have been correct when he intuitively conjectured that the pineal was the seat of the soul and served to integrate the mind with the body.

Circadian rhythms refer to the twenty-four-hour physiological cycles that all tissues and organs display. These fluctuations of metabolic activity involve every system of the body, such as brain, heart, liver, kidney, and digestive tract. Even single cells are genetically programmed to have their own internalized circadian rhythms. Individuals participating in deep cave confinement experiments, living for months in the continual absence of sunlight, clocks, or awareness of daylight, still display these circadian physiologic daily cycles. Under these circumstances the cycles usually average slightly longer, about twenty-four-and-a-half hours, so that after several weeks, they may become inverted to the natural day. So, although spontaneous circadian rhythms are programmed to approximate the natural day, it requires an awareness of natural daylight rhythms for exact correlation.

Depression, Anxiety, and Circadian Rhythms

Depression and anxiety can involve desynchronizations between normally integrated physiologic rhythms. The daily, circadian, rhythms related to variation of temperature between morning and night, with greater secretion of cortisone in the early morning hours, have been frequently demonstrated to be disrupted in depression. Similar disturbances interrupt the normal rhythm of sound sleep at night and adequate energy in the daytime, normal appetite and weight, and normal sexual activity.

Our new term, *psychometabolic rhythm*, would then describe the dual psychologic and metabolic nature of those bodily rhythms capable of influencing or being influenced by emotional reactions. These include all of the many bodily functions of the vegetative depression and anxiety psychosomatic symptoms listed in the Depression-Anxiety Chart in Chapter 3.

Similarly, the relationship between anxiety and depression could be differentiated in terms of duration and multiplicity of psychometabolic rhythm desynchronizations. Depression involves diffuse, prolonged disruptions of many psychometabolic rhythms, while anxiety tends to be more restricted to relatively few and for shorter periods of time. Some examples of anxiety could be manifest either as transient anxiety attacks of palpitation, hyperventilation, and fear, or tension headaches with anger. But depression would be likely to continue longer and include such numerous symptoms as fatigue; middle-of-the-night insomnia; combinations of guilt, fear, or anger; loss of self-esteem and meaning for life; social irritability or seclusiveness, as well as associated anxiety symptoms. This is why one should suspect and look for confirmative symptoms of depression when anxiety is unusually persistent, severe, and incapacitating.

Anxiety tends to produce its psychometabolic rhythm changes as accelerations of many bodily rhythms such as heart rate, blood pressure, and breathing rate, and also causes restless pacing, tremors, muscle spasms, diarrhea, frequent urination, and excess sweating. Anxiety's excessive secretion

of adrenalin and the sympathetic nervous activity that underlies many of these psychometabolic symptoms are themselves
abnormally excessive responses and therefore also constitute a
disturbed psychometabolic rhythm.

Desynchronization

When physical or mental activities are performed with interest and enthusiasm, an increase of energy and well-being
usually results, but when activities are done with anxiety or
boredom, they seem to result in fatigue and lowered mood. This
difference probably depends on whether synchronization in
psychometabolic rhythms is disturbed or enhanced. The close
correlation between energy and mood probably depends on
shared biochemical pathways.

Even though the conscious psychological symptoms of
depression's mood alterations—intellectual impairment, social
symptoms, reduction of self-image, and awareness of guilt,
anger, and fear—may not seem at first to be related to disturbances of bodily physiologic rhythms, they nevertheless are a
part of the same neurochemical physiology as the more physical symptoms. They also tend to fluctuate in severity during
daily or other cycles, and respond to treatment along with the
physical psychosomatic symptoms. Because they cannot as yet
be measured by objective means, most of the psychometabolic
rhythm attention will be focused on the more physical psychosomatic symptoms.

Psychometabolic rhythm desynchronization could help explain why most reactive depressions are often preceded or
accompanied by anxiety and why both these disorders often
have common precipitating events. It might also explain so-called endogenous or retardive depression where there are no
obvious, immediately preceding external psychological
stresses, and where there is usually no preceding or accompanying expression of anxiety. In endogenous depression, the
psychometabolic rhythm desynchronizations are characterized
by excessive slowing in bodily rhythms, in contrast to the accelerations that occur in anxiety with depression. Retardive
depression's slowdown in speech, thought, and bodily movement is known as psychomotor retardation. It may also involve
retardation of internal organ metabolic rhythms, resulting in
constipation, coldness, loss of appetite, slow pulse, and breathing rate.

Manic-depressive illness is the less frequent bipolar form,

where the retarded slowdown form of depression may alternate with just the opposite manic symptoms of abnormally rapid, rambling thinking and speech, hyperactive mobility and a false sense of euphoria. These opposing phases do not occur with regularity; they often have normal periods between them or at times only manifest as one or the other. In this latter circumstance, the bipolar dual underlying nature is suspected from either family history or response to lithium medication.

Since these phases of overactive mania and retarded depression usually each persist for months, they should not be confused with the normal ups and downs that affect normal mood variation and behavior. In this latter case, they usually last only hours or days and are not intense enough to significantly interfere with normal family and occupational activities. The manic phase of manic disease often involves, in addition to flight of ideas and overactivity, some degree of inappropriateness or bizarreness, so that the behavior in severe cases may occasionally simulate schizophrenia.

The system of emotional and health influences called biorhythm charts should not be confused with our discussion of physiologic and emotional psychometabolic rhythms. These biorhythm charts use the same arbitrary number of days for everyone to measure fixed intervals of time for health, emotional and intellectual cycles, beginning with one's birth date. Since we lack adequate experience with them, we can neither endorse nor refute biorhythms and so we maintain a position of skeptical openmindedness as defined in Chapter 1.

Curiously, the folk wisdom in such common everyday expressions as "I feel like I am coming apart," or "I wish I could pull myself together," suggest an early native awareness of the emotional implications of psychometabolic desynchronization. Depression and anxiety can then be understood as involving desynchronization in bodily physiologic rhythms sufficient in degree to disturb emotional health, but not severe enough to pose an immediate threat to physical survival or to cause any anatomic change.

The term *psychometabolic rhythm* is distinguished from *metabolic rhythm* in that it involves an emotional reaction and not an anatomical disease process. For example, if an otherwise healthy person had an anxiety attack, with a rapidly beating normal heart, this would be considered a psychometabolic rhythm disturbance. Someone with physical heart disease could have, of course, an abnormal heart rhythm precipitated by emotional stress, which would then involve both metabolic and psychometabolic rhythm disturbances.

Control of physiologic rhythmicity to synchronize all of the many bodily metabolic rhythms requires a system capable of detecting changes in organs all over the body, while at the same time coordinating the various functions of different organs together. Furthermore, this system must have its own centralized coordinating master rhythm pacemaker capable of adjusting to external as well as internal environmental changes vital to the survival and health of the individual.

The Synchronizer

For physiologic and anatomic reasons, we believe that this master metabolic rhythm synchronizer involves the brain stem area of the hypothalamus, pituitary, and pineal gland. This centralized coordinating system is both affected by and affects all of the emotional, psycholgical, and metabolic factors discussed in this book. This is the probable site of the moodostat or mood thermostat postulated in Chapter 4, which now can also be appreciated for its dynamic rhythmic characteristics, and is the common site where drugs, nutritional, and psychological influences may exert their effects.

The pituitary gland controls and coordinates the hormonal secretions of most of the other glands of the body by its own chemical hormone secretions, transported through the bloodstream, which in turn influence many of the endocrine metabolic functions of the body and exert feedback control upon the pituitary and and also the hypothalamus.

Neurologic brain control is coordinated in the hypothalamus of the brain adjacent to the pituitary and the thalamus, which acts like a switchboard, receiving and transmitting electrical nerve messages to and from all parts of the brain and nervous system, including those from the sensory organs, muscles, and internal organs. The hypothalamus secretes special release hormones through a special closed circulation to control the various functions of the pituitary. The intimate anatomic and physiologic relationships of the hypothalamus, pituitary, and pineal gland make them the logical sites for control of metabolic (and psychometabolic) rhythms.

This theory helps explain how such a wide variety of physical and psychological influences can affect behavior and health, and helps account for much that has been observed in this book in dealing with emotional processes. Although it doesn't provide all of the specific details yet to be learned about emotional behavior, a psychometabolic rhythm emotional concept will allow a dynamic time-related system by which to correlate both known and future information.

In support of this theory are numerous studies that report impairment in the normal hormonal responses of the pituitary after injections of specific hypothalamic hormones in those with depression. An article in *The Archives of Psychiatry* also concluded that the origin of depression may be in the derangement of pituitary responsiveness to the hypothalamus of the brain.

This approach can help explain the significant effects of the metabolic factors upon mood and health. Regular exercise, in addition to its benefit in increasing circulation and oxygen utilization, and relief of excessive muscle tension, probably serves to resynchronize a dysrhythmic mood center by the regular rhythmic training of repetitive exercise. We postulate that the repetitious muscular contractions in muscles, heart, and lungs required by walking, running, cycling, sports, and yoga resynchronize various bodily physiologic rhythms through feedback on the centralized rhythmic synchronizer described above. Stretch muscle sensors and stretch lung receptors can transmit these messages through sensory and vagus nerve fibers to the spinal cord and the brain. It is a known physiologic reflex that taking deep breaths has a slowing effect on the heart rate, and that some benefits of conditioning exercises can be explained as parasympathetic slowing in rhythms.

In the case of caffeine, alcohol, sugars, and various sedative drugs, their stimulation or sedation of certain organs more than others make their functioning desynchronous or out of phase with each other, thereby aggravating or promoting anxiety, depression, functional fatigue, and functional hypoglycemia. For example, caffeine exaggerates the metabolic activity of adrenalin to stimulate the heart rate, blood pressure, breathing rate, and mental irritability out of physiologic harmony and phase with digestion, sleep, and other bodily functions. In addition, any initial drug sedation or stimulation is often followed later by a letdown of fatigue and moodiness, which is usually not recognized as being related to the drug.

Physical and emotional illness can then be appreciated in terms of how severe and how widespread are desynchronizations between the various organs and systems of the body, not only within itself, but also in relationship to the external environment. This basic concept can hardly be considered innovative, since it was essentially taught by the father of scientific medicine—Hippocrates—over 2,000 years ago.

Theory of Depression

The commonly accepted chemical theory of depression is very compatible with this psychometabolic rhythm desynchronization theory. The theory is that acquired deficiency in brain neurotransmitter chemicals is responsible for the symptoms of depression and that brain cell transmissions are therefore impaired. The psychometabolic desynchronization theory would simply add that as a result of the lack of sufficient energy chemical transmitters, the hypothalamus brain centers lack sufficient energy neurotransmitters to synchronize the various bodily organs, the pituitary gland and its dependent endocrine glands, and perhaps the pineal.

Neurotransmitter deficiency could then be caused by any combination of psychological, environmental, drug, or physical metabolic factors, including anatomic physical illness. The two main neurotransmitter chemicals involved are serotonin and norepinephrine, and their metabolic products have been found to be reduced in certain forms of depression. Conversely, treatment with antidepressant medication or electroshock therapy has been found to restore normal levels of neurotransmitter.

An important biochemical relationship, which to our knowledge has not been dealt with to any significant degree, is that of anxiety to depression. Not only does anxiety occur in the majority of those with depression, but it often precedes it, and in our experience, seems capable of causing depression. We postulate the following mechanism, which seems to fit known biochemical facts. It has long been known that the major hormonal alteration of anxiety is the wasteful excessive secretion of epinephrine and norepinephrine into the bloodstream from the adrenal gland and sympathetic nerve endings outside of the brain. As a result, we believe that there must be some point at which long-standing or severe anxiety could deplete the brain's supply of specific norepinephrine precursor amino acids or specific required enzymes. This overutilization theory would not account for those whose depression is characterized by primarily serotonin depletion, or in those endogenous depressions where there is not obvious anxiety.

In these latter cases of depression, there may be lack of production of adequate neurotransmitter chemicals unrelated to overutilization outside of the brain. The endogenous depressions may be somehow related to the excessive parasympathetic nervous slowdown so characteristic of this form, in contrast to the sympathetic nervous system hyperactivity characteristic of those whose depression is associated with anxiety.

Metabolic rhythms can also involve anatomic physical diseases in optimal timings for therapy and medication. They may help explain why some diseases occur with greater frequency in certain seasons or times of day, and why the same dose of medication may have different therapeutic or side effects at different times. Animal experiments do suggest that this may be so, but little such investigation has been done in humans.

Awake-Sleep Cycle

The most prominent, though poorly understood, metabolic rhythm is the awake-sleep cycle. For most animals, including humans, the biologic tendency to rest and sleep during the nighttime absence of sunlight, and to be most active during the daytime presence of sunlight, is usually taken for granted. People who work during the night and sleep during the day usually require considerable time to get used to it. In a sense, they often suffer the symptoms similar to jet lag, with disturbances in energy, sleep, mood, and digestion secondary to disharmony in various bodily rhythms and functions being out of phase with each other. Most of those who have to partake of this reversal of natural rhythms never do feel completely natural with it.

This awake-sleep cycle is so fundamental to emotional health that its persistent disruption provides the two most common vegetative symptoms of depression: middle-of-the-night insomnia and lack of energy during the day. Since disruption of this awake-sleep metabolic rhythm has its most evident effects upon emotional health rather than upon physical survival, our new term *psychometabolic rhythm* seems appropriate to describe it.

Sleep has always been a subject for conjecture and awe—probably because the relative immobility and lack of responsiveness associated with it resemble death, and because of the mysterious symbolism involved in dreams. Sleep laboratory studies have disclosed that sleep normally is composed of four progressively deeper stages of sleep, detectable on the electroencephalograph. These alternate with a stage of dreaming sleep evidenced by rapid eye movements under the closed lids. This latter stage can be detected with special instruments and is appropriately known as REM sleep. The duration of one complete series of these sleep stages is about ninety minutes, and most people will experience four to six such cycles each night.

Reduction in the metabolic activities of most organs during sleep causes decreases in heart rate, breathing, blood pressure, temperature, urinary and digestive functions, and muscular movement. Exceptions, occurring during deep sleep, include the increased secretion of cortisone from the adrenal gland, growth hormone from the pituitary, and melitonin from the pineal. Although the exact neurochemical physiology that controls sleep and wakefulness remains unknown, the gradual induction of sleep through progressive stages of sleepiness and the normally gradual awakening through lighter stages of sleep strongly suggest some chemical, hormonal influence acting upon the brain. Control of sleep circadian rhythms also involves the pineal gland. Its hormone, melitonin, is closely related to serotonin, and is necessary for normal sleep.

The reduced metabolic physiology during sleep allows restoration of energy for the following day's activities. Prolonged sleep deprivation causes irritability and even hallucinations, but no one has been known to have died for lack of sleep nor have suffered more serious symptoms than profound fatigue or those mentioned above.

Function of Sleep

We theorize that the primary function of sleep is to provide resynchronization for all of the body's physiologic rhythms. We offer this theory because it would explain a system for emotional and physical restoration of such diversely operating metabolic systems as digestion, renal, cardiac, pulmonary, and mental, which have grown out of phase with each other through their individual daily physiologic demands and stresses. During sleep they can be resynchronized to their baseline states of usually minimal activity, then an energetic, composed individual with synchronized metabolic rhythms can start the next day's activities with a sense of well-being. Without this daily returning or resynchronization, the degree of disharmony between metabolic rhythms would progressively worsen day by day.

Dreaming has received much attention throughout history. Its content, emotionality, duration, and recall are influenced not only by previous wakeful experiences, but also by such metabolic influences as physical illness, fever, mood, drugs, diet, and environmental temperature. Sleep researchers agree that dreaming is necessary to help resolve emotional tension and to aid learning and memory.

Sleep Disturbances

In sleep laboratory monitoring, it has been demonstrated that depression is usually accompanied by desynchronized patterns of sleep. This includes decrease in deep stage four sleep, erratic increase or decrease in REM dreaming sleep, and loss of regularity in the rhythmic sequence of sleep cycles.

These disturbances in the normal psychometabolic rhythm of sleep help explain the nocturnal symptoms of depression and anxiety, inability to fall or stay asleep, nightmares, and morbid, fearful worrying during the hours when one should be sleeping. At the same time, they help explain not only daytime drowsiness and fatigue, but also the desynchronizations that comprise the conscious, social, and unconscious symptoms of depression.

Sleep laboratory studies have also been useful in disclosing how drugs in food, drink, and pills may affect not only sleep but also the overall depression state itself. Alcohol and barbiturate sleeping pills tend to decrease REM and deep stage four sleep. Use of these drugs, especially in larger doses, can at times cause early-morning insomnia or worsening of depression, and may require weeks after their withdrawal to obtain normal sleep patterns.

In our clinical experience with caffeine, as little as a single cup of coffee or tea in the morning can result in severe insomnia at night for those so predisposed. Alcohol, barbiturates, many sleeping pills, and some tranquilizers can aggravate depression, while antidepressant medication has been shown to normalize sleep patterns in quality and amount of sleep.

Heart Rhythm

Since earliest times the heart has been regarded as the "seat of the soul" or emotional center. Most likely this is because of the heartbeat's prompt reaction to any strong emotional stimulus with readily detectable changes in its intensity, rate, and regularity of rhythm. When due to emotional stimulation in a normal heart, this type of palpitation is often frightening, though harmless. If the emotional experience is one of joy, such as love, the palpitation would usually be thought of as part of a pleasant sensation. The folklore of common language has produced terms such as *stout-hearted, black-hearted* and *faint-hearted* to signify a wide variety of emotional characteristics attributed to heart rhythm responses.

Brain Rhythm

The metabolic rhythm of the brain's electrical activity, as recorded in the electroencephalograph, might have been expected to provide the most important clues to diagnosing emotional illnesses but this has not yet been the case, although it has been useful for diagnosing seizure disorders and physical brain diseases, as well as studying stages of sleep and relaxation states. Perhaps this limitation is related to the emotional center's deep position within the brain near the hypothalamus; the clinical practicality of electroencephalography is restricted to detecting changes at the superficial cortex of the brain. One uncommon form of seizure, called a psychomotor seizure, does involve behavioral changes and may be diagnosed by the electroencephalograph. In recent years comparisons in voltages of brain waves between the two sides of the brain have helped us understand which side of the brain is more involved in intellectual, verbal functions (left side for right-handed people), and which side is most involved in intuitive, spontaneous, creative, and spatial relationships (right side in right-handed people).

The Price of Ignoring Our Rhythms

Our modern, time-pressured, fractionated way of life has been a major contributor to the epidemic of anxiety and depression in modern societies. What is a more appropriate way to understand this relationship than as the continuing conflict between the synchronizing capacity of natural human beings and the artificial demands of modern life-styles?

Disregard of human health limitations is evident everywhere: rushing to maintain tight occupational, social, and personal time schedules; disregarding appropriate time for adequate sleep at night, allowing inadequate time for the eating of what should be more natural foodstuffs; and maintaining a life-style based on drugs, food, and drink ingredients to help wake us up, put us to sleep, relax us, stimulate us, enhance sexual response and make us more sociable. Every phase of human psychologic and physiologic activity is now under artificial time schedules that ignore natural ones. Psychometabolic rhythms once tuned to the earth's rotation on its axis for daytime activities and nighttime sleep are now disregarded in favor of artificial lighting, jet travel, and pressure to succeed by overwork and oversocialization far into the night.

Throughout the history of human behavior, as evident in literature, we note the longing to return to more natural lifestyles and surroundings for the relief of depression. Ishmael seeks to escape his depression in *Moby Dick* by going to sea. Since Hippocrates, physicians have recommended going to the seashore, mountains, or woods in an effort to restore health.

The Psychometabolic Rhythm Concept

In summary, the psychometabolic rhythm concept offers a common basis for understanding the interaction between psychological and physiological processes that result in human emotional experiences. It allows a time-related perspective for differentiating health from disease, based on whether or not there is normal synchronization between all of the various organs, within the cells of each organ, and between the intact individual with his or her ever-changing environment. Furthermore, this concept allows insight into the dynamic interrelationship between rhythmic events of the external physical world and those of the internal biologic system.

Psychometabolic rhythm synchronization also offers more closely defined, tangible, and measurable means with which to pursue future research, education, and treatment for emotional problems. This approach helps to unravel the seeming contradiction that all life processes are constantly changing but at the same time repetitious. And finally, this innovative but speculative concept seems a fitting subject on which to end a book whose primary emphasis has been on continuity and integration.